Dirty Shorts
Volume One

By Kyle Adams

Dirty Shorts Volume One

Published by Kyle Adams

All Stories Copyright© 2013 by Kyle Adams

All rights reserved.

ISBN 9781304338914

License Notes

Book Contents

Introduction to Love Has No Boundaries

The story you are about to read celebrates love, sex and romance between men. It is a product of the *Love Has No Boundaries* promotion sponsored by the *Goodreads M/M Romance Group* and is published as a free gift to you.

What Is Love Has No Boundaries?

The Goodreads M/M Romance Group invited members to choose a photo and pen a letter asking for a short M/M romance story inspired by the image; authors from the group were encouraged to select a letter and write an original tale. The result was an outpouring of creativity that shone a spotlight on the special bond between M/M romance writers and the people who love what they do.

A written description of the image that inspired this story is provided along with the original request letter. If you'd like to view the photo, please feel free to join the Goodreads M/M Romance Group and visit the discussion section: *Love Has No Boundaries.*

Photo Description

A young man is trimming his hedges wearing only a pair of dirty jeans showing off his muscular body.

Story Letter

Dear Author,

I saw this guy every Saturday last spring and summer during my routine trash pickup route in his neighborhood. I could never find the courage to speak to him. I feel like something keeps pulling me towards him. How can I approach him? What will he think of me... a garbage man?

Sincerely,

Gina

DIRTY BOYS

By Kyle Adams

"You've got it bad, Devon," Mark said, loud enough that I could hear him over the engine noise emitting from the garbage truck.

I shrugged off his comment and only responded with a casual, "Whatever."

Mark is my best friend and coworker. We are waste collectors, more commonly known as garbage men. We have been lucky enough to be on the same route for almost seven years now, since I started with the company at eighteen, right after graduating high school. Mark was a few years older than I was, but we became fast friends. Working with Mark made the monotonous job almost enjoyable. It wasn't all bad, but it would have been very repetitive without Mark's companionship. I won't lie, sometimes there are nasty surprises waiting inside the trashcans, but mostly it isn't too bad. Dale, the driver for our route, wasn't bad either, but I didn't know him that well, as we did not have as many opportunities to talk like Mark and I did. Mark and I spent a lot of time hanging onto the back of the truck and chatting with each other, which helped distract us from the worst of the horrors lurking inside barrels with poorly-bagged garbage.

I finished returning the now-empty trashcan to the sidewalk in front of our current stop— Connor's well-landscaped home. Connor is the most gorgeous man I've ever seen. I learned his name when he moved in last summer and the recycling container I delivered had his name on the paperwork.

I took my time, wanting to get one last glimpse of him. He was mowing his lawn and not paying attention to the people picking up his trash. Why would he? I couldn't help but admire his taut ass as he pushed the mower in the opposite direction of me. His back muscles stretched the fabric of his red T-shirt. His jeans hugged every inch of his muscular legs all the way up to that *stunning* ass.

I'd give anything to bury my cock in his ass. I knew that one fuck would leave me wanting more, but I'd settle for just once. I was really looking for a relationship, but I wasn't so delusional that I didn't realize it was less likely to happen than winning the lottery. I've never even spoken to him, and I knew I was dreaming when I thought about trying to start something with him. He lived in a nice house, in a nice quiet neighborhood. I was only the garbage man who lived in a small apartment too close to the train tracks. It was clean and affordable though, and while the trains were loud at first, I got used to the noise after a couple months.

If only I could somehow find the nerve to approach him. All last summer I watched him work in his yard. It was the highlight of my Saturday mornings, seeing him tending his lawn, often only half-dressed. In the fall, I'd wait all week just to get a glimpse of him raking leaves or bundling sticks. And winter! Not only was it the worst season for a man in my business, weather-wise, but it was also the time of year when most people disappeared indoors. And stayed there. Unfortunately for me, Connor was no different. Those few occasions when I caught glimpses of him getting in his car over the long cold months were like rays of sunshine.

But, who was I kidding? If, by some miracle, he was even gay, he would most certainly never want the trash man. At least it was now spring again, and I'd get to see more of him. I'm not sure what it says about me that my attraction to him has lasted through all the seasons. I'm starting to think I'll never get over it.

"You have it even worse than I thought." I heard Mark speak, and it drew me back into the present. I turned away from Connor just as he was getting ready to loop around pushing his mower in my direction.

- 6 -

Looking up to meet Mark's eyes, I replied casually but loud enough to be heard, "I'm not sure what you mean."

"Please, you're totally smitten." I gave him my best "you're crazy" stare.

He was, of course, unfazed and continued with his explanation, "Look at the previous guy's can." Mark pointed towards the house whose trash we'd just emptied. "It's fucking rolling down the sidewalk and is almost in the street. While" —he stopped to point at Connor's waste bin— "Pretty boy's container, you've all but put it away for him."

I figured that if Connor saw Mark waving his hands, he would assume Mark was yelling at me about something. I was relieved that he wouldn't hear what Mark actually said over the truck and his lawn mower.

I didn't look back at Connor's cans because I knew they were where they were supposed to be. "It's not my fault they," I waved my hand in the direction of the fallen container, "bought cheap trash cans that can't stay upright and roll easy," I said, as I hopped up onto the truck where Mark was already waiting. The truck took off, and it was conveniently too noisy to talk easily.

Unfortunately, at the next stop, Mark started the conversation back up right where he left off. "You should talk to him. Ask him out." He said it encouragingly, and not for the first time.

Yeah, like it was that easy. He was always telling me to at least wave or nod if I wouldn't say anything. Sometimes he would even try coaching me in what to say: "Tell him you like his primed *rosebuds*." He winked at me. Ever since he heard rosebud was a synonym for asshole, he liked to say it as lewdly and as often as possible.

"I don't even know if he is gay," I muttered.

"He's gay." Mark sounded certain.

"How do you know?" I asked skeptically.

"I have excellent gaydar." Mark smiled smugly.

"You're not even gay," I pointed out.

"You don't have to be gay to have a solidly functioning gaydar detection system." Mark carelessly slung the can he was finished dumping back onto the sidewalk. "I've seen him looking at you too, the same way you look at him," Mark said, as we jumped back on the truck heading to the next house.

Jumping off the truck at the next stop, I asked Mark, "What look is that?"

"You know, the I-want-you-so-so-bad-but-I'm-too-chicken-shit-to-even-say-hi look."

That was the first time Mark had said that he'd seen Connor looking at me. I felt my heart falter as I allowed myself to feel that maybe Connor was attracted to me too, if only for a brief moment. *Doubtful*, I thought. Mark must have been reading Connor wrong. I forced myself to finish the job at hand, returning the bin I'd just emptied to the sidewalk and jumping up on the truck. I knew Mark was right about me acting scared. I wasn't convinced Connor was giving me the same look, though. Either way, I didn't have anything else to say to Mark about it.

I pretended I didn't hear him when he again yelled across the truck. "Seriously, if you won't talk to him, I'm going to do it for you."

****

The next Saturday...

Connor wasn't wearing a shirt today, just a pair of loose and really dirty jeans with a sleek black belt keeping them up on his waist. He was using a hedge trimmer that showed off his muscular arms as he held it up to the shrubs. He had a full pack of ab muscles and well-defined pecs with perfect small brown nipples. His light brown hair was a short buzz-cut that looked really good on him. Not for the first time, I imagined how our bodies would feel against each other. I was a little taller and a little wider than he was. My body was in good shape. I had strong arms and shoulders, but my stomach wasn't quite as ripped as Connor's killer six-pack.

I emptied Connor's can and returned it to the curb as slowly and quietly as I could, trying not to draw attention to my actions. I wanted all the time I could get to admire Connor's perfect body, but didn't want to be caught doing it. Connor in action was something I would never forget. When I finally turned around to hop back on the truck, I came face to face with Mark.

Rubbing his shoulder and neck, Mark said, "Switch sides with me." He started slowly rolling his shoulder up and down. "My left side feels tight, and I need to hold on with my right."

I nodded my agreement and started to step past Mark to get to the other side. I looked back over at Connor, and saw he had turned off the hedge cutter and was setting it on the ground. When he looked up, our eyes connected. I felt a moment of panic being caught looking, but it quickly faded as my foot suddenly caught on something and I nose-dived into the pavement. At that point, all I felt was sheer humiliation. I wasn't sure if Mark had tripped me or if I stumbled over my own feet. I didn't really care at the moment. I just wanted to get up before Connor noticed that I fell like a clumsy fool. I groaned, remembering that we had been looking at each other when I fell, so there was no way Connor hadn't noticed. *Fucking fantastic.*

Laughing, Mark said, "Watch where you're walking there, buddy." He followed it up with more laughter.

I started to push myself up, when a firm hand gripped my arm and helped pull me to my feet.

"Are you okay?" Connor asked, keeping a hold of my arm as if he was worried I might fall again.

I opened my mouth to say something, though I wasn't quite sure what, but Connor didn't give me the chance to speak. "Maybe you should sit down until we're sure you're okay."

"You're right," Mark chimed in, appearing on my other side and feigning concern before Connor could try to make me sit down. I glared at him, not sure what he was up to. "We can't wait for Devon though, we have got to go empty the truck, and it'll take at least ninety minutes. Can you stay with him, and we'll come back and pick him up after dumping this load and refueling?" Mark phrased it as a question, but his tone didn't leave any room for refusal.

My glare deepened, and I knew I was probably looking at Mark like I wanted to kill him. Before I could say I was okay and that the truck wasn't full or needing gas, Connor responded, "Of course, I'll make sure he's taken care of."

"Thank you," Mark told Connor before leaning into my ear and whispering, "You'll thank me for this later."

The last time he said those words to me, I ended up being robbed when he and his wife had taken me out to my first gay bar for my twenty-first birthday. Yadda yadda, I woke up to find my shit, which I had cleverly hidden in the oven, gone. It was not a fun experience, and I still blamed Mark for that disaster to this day.

"I'm Connor, by the way," he said, as the truck pulled away, leaving us standing in the street.

Even though he wasn't looking at me, I smiled and said "Devon. Nice to meet you."

****

When Connor then spoke the words, "Let's get you inside and cleaned up," I had a feeling Mark was right. Connor led me toward his house, and as I glanced back at the truck fading into the distance, I thought I might end up actually owing Mark for this one. I might even have to forgive him a little for the birthday disaster. Maybe.

As much as I wanted to go inside with Connor, I felt bad for troubling him. He hadn't sounded put out or inconvenienced when he spoke earlier, but just in case, I offered him an out. "I'll be okay if you're busy. You don't have to stop your work to help me."

Connor's pale blue eyes met mine. "I was already done with trimming the bushes, and I'm not just going to leave you out here waiting for them to come back."

He pulled my arm towards his house. I glanced down at his hand, realizing that before, so much was happening that I really didn't notice how warm his hand was, or how good it felt against my arm. I was so distracted thinking about how that hand would feel wrapped around a different part of my body that I wasn't paying attention to the fact that I was letting him guide me. Unfortunately, I failed to see the curb and stumbled forward. I would have fallen again, but Connor had quick reflexes. He brought his free hand up to my chest and kept me from completely losing my balance.

"You okay?" His voice showed his worry. He left his hand on my chest, and I was afraid he could feel my heart pounding like a jackhammer.

I felt my face flush, and I wasn't sure if it was more from embarrassment or a reaction to the intimate contact. My cock was more than half-hard, so I must not have been too embarrassed.

"I'm not usually so clumsy," I said weakly. I really didn't want Connor thinking I was a total klutz, but it was probably a little too late for that.

"I'm sure, but you did just fall down. Are you dizzy or anything?" Connor asked, sounding concerned, though he didn't falter at all leading me towards his house. I made sure to look where I was walking as we continued on toward his porch.

"Seriously, Connor, I'm fine."

"You're not actually. You have a cut above your eye."

It must have been the adrenaline rush, or my near panic and embarrassment, because I had not realized that I had cut myself. It couldn't have been very deep or I would have felt it bleeding.

"Thank you again for helping me; sorry my friend just *dumped* me on you," I said, trying to make a little joke.

"That's okay, I love a good dump," Connor said automatically.

I couldn't help but stop walking and laugh. I looked at him and his cheeks turned a little red, so I tried to stop laughing.

"That didn't come out right. I meant that to sound a little flirty, not gross."

I didn't know what to make of Connor's revelation. Did he really want to flirt with me, or had he just said that as an excuse? If he *had* been flirting, then maybe if I played my cards right, he would end up doing more than just flirt.

When we reached the steps leading up to his front door, he paused. As I looked at him, he was nervously biting his bottom lip.

"Seriously, I can walk up the stairs by myself. I'm fine, really," I said, saving him from having to ask whatever he was biting his lip to avoid. To demonstrate, I casually shrugged out of his grip and walked up the two steps without stumbling once. Smiling triumphantly, I raised both hands and said, "See?"

"I'm sorry. I'm overreacting. Seeing you fall just freaked me out I guess." Connor walked past me to open the front door.

Stepping inside, I toed off my boots, peeled the gloves off my hands, and took off my bright reflective vest, leaving it all just inside his front door. I followed him inside, looking around at the clean house. I surreptitiously sniffed myself. Thankfully, I didn't smell. At least I didn't think I did. I said a word of thanks that there hadn't been any accidents or broken bags this morning. Thank God, it wasn't one of those days where I was hit with some unidentifiable substance shooting out of the crusher.

Connor led me through his comfortably decorated living room and into the kitchen. He pulled one of the chairs out from his round, wooden table and turned it to face the room. "Go ahead and sit here while I run and grab some supplies," he said, as he walked out of the room.

I took the opportunity to wash my hands in the sink, as I hadn't realized they'd gotten so sweaty. I imagine that had more to do with being so close to Connor than because of the gloves. They were used to the gloves.

I was sitting in the high-back chair by the time Connor returned. At first, he looked relieved that I was still there, like I would actually leave. But then his face shifted into a smile sweet enough to make my insides melt. The fluttering in my stomach had nothing to do with the embarrassment I'd felt earlier and everything to do with the way Connor was currently looking at me. I really liked how eager he was to take care of me, even if I wasn't really hurt.

****

He set his first aid kit on the table, pulling out what he needed. Turning to face me, he opened an antiseptic pad. I was already looking up at him, but he still put his hand under my chin to tilt my head further back. I could feel the warmth of his hand all the way to my toes. His grip was firm but gentle, and although it wasn't sexual, his touch made my cock even harder in my jeans. "This might sting," he warned.

"It's okay, I'm a big boy," I said playfully, looking him in the eyes.

He licked his lips and said in a low voice I almost didn't hear, "I just bet you are." He pressed the pad to my forehead above my left eyebrow, and I flinched and closed my eyes. It wasn't too painful, just burned a little.

A few minutes later, after he finished cleaning and then putting a bandage over the scratch, he asked, "Were you hurt anywhere else?" He let his gaze travel down my body, and I knew he saw my hard-on when his eyes widened a little.

I realized I was holding my breath as I watched him swallow. I had trouble taking my eyes off his throat, but eventually our gazes met. He'd already seen my obviously-aroused cock, but my desire and willingness must have been readable in my expression because his smile spread sensually across his face.

It must have been all he needed to know, as seconds later he was dropping down between my spread legs, resting his hands on my lower thighs. Looking back up at me, he said, "Did you scrape your knees or anything?"

I gently shook my head, letting him know my knees were fine, if you didn't count the anxious shaking he undoubtedly felt. "So, there is nothing else I can help you take care of?" he practically purred, letting his eyes drift down to the bulge of my hard cock pressing against my jeans.

His hands very slowly slid up my thighs, and I watched as he licked his bottom lip. "I wouldn't be a very good nursemaid if I didn't make sure you were fully taken care of. And it looks like you have some swelling I could help alleviate."

"Okay," I said hoarsely. My brain was pretty much short-circuiting at this point. I may not have been formulating sentences, but I knew what Connor was offering, and no way would I say no.

He didn't waste any time getting my jeans undone and fishing my hard cock out of my boxers. "Beautiful," he said appreciatively, stroking my throbbing erection from base to tip in a tantalizingly slow movement. I bit the side of my thumb trying to distract myself from how embarrassingly close to coming I already was.

Thankfully, Connor didn't notice. He seemed to be in a trance, watching the head of my cock disappear and reemerge through his fist. A few slow jerks later and he looked up, giving me a devilish smile. "I *was* going to taste you." I moaned at the images his words sparked, and then he continued. "But I think I have a better idea." He finished his sentence by letting go of my cock and standing up. "It involves at least one of us getting naked."

"That" —I swallowed— "sounds like an amazing idea."

"Yeah?" he asked, slowly starting to roll his hips, tracing his hand across his denim-covered erection. "Since I'm already half way there," he purred, slowly unhooking his belt and unsnapping his jeans, "and you have to go back to work…" He lowered his zipper sinfully slow. "I figured it should be me."

"Even better," I said breathlessly, unable to take my eyes off him.

He grinned, but said nothing as he continued to shimmy his hips to the teasingly seductive rhythm he had set. Spinning around, he hooked both sides of his jeans with his thumbs and slowly lowered them over his firm, rounded cheeks. He had on pink boxer briefs that were tight enough for me to see his ass dimples. If he had been performing his strip tease any closer, I would have reached out and squeezed them, but for now, I had to be content with just looking.

"Come here," I quietly stated, trying to sound commanding but sounding more desperate instead. He just smiled and shook his head while continuing his erotic dance. "Please?" I practically begged, badly wanting to touch him.

Grinning over his shoulder, he said, "Not yet."

"Tease." I meant to say it playfully, but it came out a growl.

He let his pants drop and kicked them away before turning back towards me wearing just his underwear. I could see his cock was equally as hard as mine, and he had a nice wet spot spreading across the material.

I licked my lips, wanting to suck my way to his luscious cock right through the thin cotton covering it.

I knew this was Connor's show, though. He was the one with the courage to initiate everything; I could wait and let him continue to do it his way. His very slow, but extremely sexy, way. God, the sensual way he moved! I could watch him grind his hips all day.

I couldn't contain my low moan when he pulled his waistband forward, letting his dick snap up and smack his stomach just below his bellybutton. The string of pre-come connecting his cock head with the briefs snapped as he continued lowering his undies. When he revealed his low-hanging balls, my mouth watered. The man I'd been fantasizing about for almost a year was standing before me in all of his glory, and I wanted to touch and lick every amazing inch of him. Still, I managed to stay in my chair not moving, not even touching my own cock, waiting for Connor to decide when it was time to take this to the next level.

Dropping his underwear, he strode toward me with a comfortable confidence that showed he knew how badly I ached for him. "Lower your pants," he said.

Obediently, I lifted my butt off the chair and pulled my jeans and boxers down towards my knees. I was going to slip them completely off, but suddenly ended up with a lap full of Connor. He straddled my legs, positioning himself so our cocks could rub together. "Better get your shirt out of the way, too," he said, grabbing the bottom of my shirt and lifting it over my head, hooking it behind my neck. It was tight, but not restricting, and it did leave my stomach and chest exposed. "Mmm," he hummed appreciatively, thrusting his erection gently against mine while he started rubbing my nipples.

My hands instinctively grabbed his ass, squeezing and caressing. Finally being able to feel him satisfied a craving that had been building since the first time I saw him. He smiled down at me, looking into my eyes as he spit into his right hand, sliding his left hand up to rest on my shoulder. Wrapping his fingers around my shaft, he slowly stroked up and down, spreading his slick spit evenly. Keeping our gazes locked, I spit into my own hand and started rubbing his engorged member.

He closed the short distance between us and crushed his lips against mine. The kiss was sloppy and wet, tongues tangling in and out of each other's mouth. His hand jerking my cock sped up, and I increased my speed to match. His passion and vigor was sensational, and too pleasurable for me to hold off climaxing. I pulled back from the kiss to grunt, "I'm coming." Moaning, I shot ropes of come on my chest and stomach. My hand stroking him faltered, but once I recovered from my release, I picked my pace back up.

I took my other hand off his backside and pressed my middle finger into Connor's mouth. He sucked gently, and after he got it nice and wet, I returned it to his ass, running my wet finger down his crack. I gently rubbed it against his opening a few times, before slowly pushing inside his tight body, while with my other hand I massaged the underside of his head with my thumb on each upward stroke. His loud moaning and mantra of, "Please don't stop, never stop, I'm almost there," along with his closed eyes and expression of total bliss, encouraged me to start thrusting into him, fucking him with my finger while simultaneously working his cock over the edge.

His release mixed with my own on my chest, but I didn't mind. I felt amazing, invigorated, and ready for another round in a few minutes. Connor, on the other hand, looked dreamily content and ready for a nap. He stretched and reached for something on the table behind me. Bringing a handful of paper towels back, he quickly wiped away the evidence of our orgasms and tossed the used towels towards his trashcan. I knew I'd be smiling and remembering this when I emptied that trash next week.

I was surprised when instead of jumping off my lap, he let his head fall onto the junction between my neck and shoulder. I felt his lips press gentle kisses against my skin. One hand I left caressing his ass; the other I rubbed along his back, just enjoying how his body felt as I held him close.

I wasn't sure how long we stayed like that, when it dawned on me that he probably had other things he needed to do, and I had no idea how soon Mark would be back. This also reminded me that I definitely needed to thank Mark for pushing us together. With my hand wrapped around Connor's lower back, I squeezed him once before murmuring, "You probably need to get back to your yard work."

"I have a confession to make." I felt him smile against my shoulder. "I hate yard work. I only do it so I can see you." His body felt good relaxed and snuggled against me. I liked that he wanted to cuddle and wasn't in a rush to separate. "Looks like I might have drooled on your shirt a little." I was pleased when he didn't pull away from me like I expected him to.

"Really?" I asked with disbelief clear in my voice.

"Just a little, though you probably won't be able to tell it's wet."

"I meant, you really only do yard work to see me?"

"Are you kidding? You're so hot. I was frustrated that I couldn't find excuses to be outside during the winter. I even tried shoveling the sidewalks when it snowed, but the neighbor's kid always conned me into paying him to do it." He sounded exasperated, but there was affection in his voice when he talked about the boy from next door.

"Why didn't you ever say anything— if you were interested in me that is?" I asked with genuine curiosity.

"You always seemed busy, and I didn't know if you'd like me hitting on you while you were working. Why didn't *you* say anything?"

"You always seemed busy, too." I tried fibbing, though he *had* been busy. At his snort, I could tell he didn't quite believe me. So I was honest. "I didn't think you would be interested in a garbage man."

Connor smiled and gave me a quick kiss. "That never bothered me for a second. Besides, I bet I'll never have to worry about you forgetting to take out the trash."

I smiled back at him and gave a cheesy reply, "I promise I'll always take the trash out as long as you promise to always mow shirtless."

"It's a deal." He smiled and leaned down to gently press his lips to mine. I could feel his answering promise in his soft kiss.

THE END

"I need your help, Leia," I pleaded, watching her closely to gauge her reaction. Nothing, not even a muscle twitch, she had perfected the art of ignoring me. "This is serious, I think I really messed up." She at least lifted her gaze to mine acknowledging my presence, but I could tell her thoughts were elsewhere. She would probably rather be outside playing ball than sitting here listening to me. "What happened? You ask." My voice dripped with sarcasm. "Thanks for your concern. I got pulled over this afternoon." Leia was watching me with what I could tell was only feigned interest. "When the officer approached the window, he said 'Papers' and before he could finish, I shouted, 'Scissors! I win,' and drove off." I waited a moment for the impact of that to sink in to her pretty little head.

Leia continued looking at me as if *I* was the idiot, but she was the one who I often caught with drool dripping down her chin. "Why did I do it? That's the stupid part. I saw it on a T-shirt, and it just popped in my head. Before I knew it, my tires were kicking gravel back at the cop. When I glanced in my rearview mirror, he just stood there looking astounded." I explained to Leia. She sighed, but I knew that sigh really meant 'you're pathetic.' I ignored her. If I wasn't in such desperate need of her help, I wouldn't have even bothered. "You have no idea what it's like in that type of situation; on the front line, survival instincts kick in, and mine screamed, 'hit the gas, motherfucker!'"

Leia just rolled onto her back, looking at me with her big, brown, puppy eyes. "What do you know anyway, you sniff your own butt and would happily eat your own poop if I didn't stop you!" I chastised her, but started rubbing her soft belly so she'd know I didn't really mean it. "Seriously though, I need you on my side for this one. Daddy Brayden loves you more than me, so if you could break the news to him, that would be great." Leia didn't look like she was on board with the plan, so I sweetened the deal, "I'll buy you a new squeaky toy. That's a sweet deal. You would be a fool not to take this." I tried to make my voice as enticing as I could, knowing my tone might help persuade her to seeing things my way.

It definitely got her attention, as she rolled back over and sat up, her little tail going back and forth. She was so adorable, you'd never suspect that beneath all of that cuteness there was a manipulative mastermind preparing for galactic domination. I knew there was nothing I could do to stop her, so I just tried to remain mostly on her good side. Then, when she assembled her empire, she might take mercy on me. Until that day came, I just tried to live life normally. Now that I had her attention, I told her the details of my plan and her role. "I was thinking I'd leave the closet open, and you could chew up a pair of daddy's favorite shoes, you know, to take the heat off of me." I could tell by the way her tail stopped wagging she wasn't going for this plan. "You know he'll never stay mad at you! But me, I'll be in the doghouse for weeks." I tried to reason with her. When Brayden came home, he would look at me and just know I'd done something. Sometimes I accused him of being a mind reader, but he always swore he wasn't telepathic, he just knew me too well.

In the end, I gave up on convincing Leia for help. She was too much of a daddy Brayden's girl, and I was just the person that followed her around, serving her food and picking up her poop. Well, if she wouldn't help me, I had other things I could do to prepare for his welcome home. I had the perfect new toy to try out too. I just hoped he'd like it.

****

A few hours later, there was a knock on the front door. I am one of those people that never looked through the peephole before opening the door. Brayden was always telling me to check before opening the door, but something about the way it was called a 'peephole' creeped me out. I told him if he wanted me to check that first, he could install a new door with a window. Since that hasn't happened, I guess he isn't too concerned about me one day opening the door to a machete-wielding lunatic. I didn't hear Leia, she must still be sleeping in the bedroom.

I wasn't surprised to see the cop standing there, but if I had looked first, I probably would have pretended not to be home, just to see what he'd do. Could not answering the door get me into more trouble than I was already in? I didn't think it would, but who knows. Avoid problems until they go away, that's a good motto. The cop just stood there looking smug with his short, but artfully messy hair and his big 'I'm hot shit' aviator, mirror glasses. Okay, truthfully, he was drop-down, flop around, piss the floor from the seizure he induced, sexy. From the way he stood there looking all confident, and maybe even a little pissed off, I could tell he knew it too.

Lowering his sunglasses, he asked, "Remember me?"

"You do have one of those faces that look familiar." I brought my hand up to my chin and pretended to think about it. "Are you the guy from the grocery store? Did I run into you with my cart?" I asked innocently. "I sure am sorry about that and promise it won't happen again." I made a 'cross my heart' gesture. "I've already signed up for cart pushing education classes and everything." Giving him my sweetest smile, I said, "Thanks for stopping by, ta-ta." I waved and started shutting the door.

He slammed his hand against the door, preventing me from closing it, he took a step forward so he was inside the doorway. "Try again." He was starting to sound irritated.

I tried using more force to close the door, but he blocked it with his boot. His big, solid boot. Big hands, big feet, one big sexy fucking package. If I had not been trying to keep him out, I'd probably take a play from Leia's book and start drooling all over myself.

"Stop trying to close the door." He growled at me. It was a deep, throaty, purely animalistic sound. As much as it intimidated me, it turned me on even more.

"You told me to try again, so I did." I let go of the door and crossed my arms over my chest defiantly. He might be a big, strong, sex god, but I was stubborn, and this was my house.

"I meant guess again, but you know what? Forget it." He stepped fully into the entryway and shut the door behind him. "You'd just make up another story, so I'll tell you who I am. I'm the cop you skipped out on, leaving me coughing in your dust like an idiot. I missed my quota for giving traffic violations because of you." His voice got lower with each word, and he was showing a mouthful of teeth, but he wasn't smiling. Well, maybe it could be a smile. In the way a hyena smiles at prey before devouring it.

"Oh, there's obviously been a mistake. I let my neighbor borrow my car earlier; he's a good person, just a bit irresponsible sometimes. I'll talk to him about it and make sure he sends you a letter of apology. You may leave now, knowing everything has been resolved."

"It was you. I'd know your mouth anywhere." He stepped toward me, forcing me to scoot back until I was touching the wall.

"Fine, it was me, but you're exaggerating. I was barely going over the suggested speed." I said sweetly. I wished I had big puppy dog eyes I could flash to always get my way.

"It's not a suggested speed, it's a limit, and seventy-seven in a fifty-five is unacceptable." He pulled his sunglasses off, putting them in his pocket.

- 23 -

"I thought you'd pulled me over for a game of Rock-Paper-Scissors, which I won. I knew you'd pick paper, it was such an obvious choice."

"I never said paper. I started to tell you why I'd pulled you over, but you cut me off and started screaming something about scissors. Then you peeled out back onto the street, where you drove off like a maniac." He shook his head. "I've never seen anything like it, and I've been a cop for six years."

"I heard you say paper." I stuck with my story. "And I've been hearing perfectly for twenty-three years, so I have more experience with this situation than you."

"I never said that." Did he always sound this angry with innocent bystanders? Why are cops always so angry whenever they talk to me? I made a mental note to write to the station and suggest all officers be forced to get relaxing, therapeutic massages at least weekly.

"Guess we had a failure to communicate." I shrugged, "Either way," I squinted at his name badge. "Officer Hendricks, I had places to be and couldn't just wait there; you understand, right?" I patted him on the chest in a goodbye gesture.

"I understand you owe me." He pressed closer, his leg slipping between mine.

"You can't be in here without a warrant." I said weakly. His hands went to the wall on both sides of my shoulders, caging me.

"I'm off duty."

"You're still in uniform." I nervously licked my bottom lip and watched as his eyes tracked my tongue's movement.

"I can change that." He started to slowly unbutton his uniform shirt while his thigh continued to rub between my legs.

"What exactly do you want?" I asked, starting to feel a little nervous.

"Fleeing and evading is a felony." He stepped back enough to grab my waist and flip me around face first against the wall. I may have squeaked from the suddenness of the move. He used enough force to show me he was in charge, but not enough to hurt. He used his feet to spread my legs and bringing my wrists together against my lower back, he held them there with one hand. It all happened so quickly that I didn't even have a chance to try and resist. "I could arrest you." He stated while using his free hand to pat me down. First my sides and then he moved to my front. He reached my cock, "Are you carrying a concealed weapon? Oh, it looks like you're just happy to see me. Very happy judging from how hard you are." He moved his hand around to my ass and squeezed. "I'm not going to arrest you, because, like I already told you, ya owe me, and I'm here to collect." He pressed his crotch into my ass, leaving no doubt what he was implying. Then I felt cool metal circle my wrists as he clicked his cuffs into place. "I'm going to need both hands for this next part."

He slipped one hand around my waist so his fingers were spread on my flat stomach and pulled me tight against his hard groin. I knew it was probably the wrong way to feel, but I'd never been more turned on in my life. "First, we're going to let your hair down," he grabbed my ponytail and pulled the black band free. My hair fell down to just past my shoulders, what I considered the prefect length; still easy to care for, with enough length for a guy to wrap around his fist, like the cop behind me was currently doing. Using his hold on my hair, he angled my head back and started kissing me. It was rough, demanding, pure pleasure I could feel down to my toes. Sucking my lower lip between his teeth, he bit down a few times, nibbling on the sensitive flesh before his tongue was demanding entrance into my mouth. Out of stubbornness I tried to deny him access, keeping my lips locked together, but he tightened his hold on my hair, making my gasp. Without wasting any time, he started thrusting his tongue into my mouth. He tongue fucked my mouth with a passion I've never felt before.

The intensity of the kiss left me dizzy, unable to wrap my head around what was happening. But my body was lit with desire, and my dick was straining against my jeans. He slipped his hand down and started fumbling with the button of my pants. Pulling out of the kiss, he growled with frustration and let go of my hair so he could use both hands to work on popping my button free. "When I pulled you over, my first thought was what it would feel like grabbing your hair and shoving my cock through your luscious lips. I planned to fuck your mouth until I exploded down your throat." He finished unfastening my jeans and started to lower them, noticing that I wasn't wearing underwear. "Then you fucking left me standing there with my cock achingly hard. You know how much that pissed me off? A lot, but it also increased my desire to track you down and fuck you senseless, which wasn't hard since I had your license plate."

I couldn't help but moan when he ran his finger down the seam of my ass, pausing when he reached my entrance. "What's this? Do you have a sex toy in here? You came home and got ready for me? That's fucking hot!" He said biting my ear.

"It wasn't for you," I mumbled weakly.

"Doesn't matter," he said, smacking my ass. "When I'm done plowing this ass," he spanked my other cheek, "You'll never be able to be fucked by anyone else again without thinking of me and what I'm about to do to you." His voice was filled with promise that left me with no doubt he meant every word. "Don't move." He grumbled as he slipped away from pressing against me.

I heard the rustling of fabric and then a thud as I think he dropped his utility belt. He stood too far back and was out of my view. I really wished I could see him stripping, even though it sounded like he was removing everything very quickly. I knew it would be hot to watch.

I didn't hear or see him return. Suddenly, without warning I felt his teeth sink into my ass. The bite was hard enough to leave an imprint in my cheek for over a week. It stung, and I grunted, but he quickly soothed the sting by licking the mark. He spread my legs as wide apart as my jeans would allow, causing my chest to slide along the wall. Thankfully, I still had on my t-shirt, which helped blocked most of the scraping against the plaster.

I lost track of all conscious thought, and my body felt like little more than a pleasure vessel when he grabbed the base of the well-lubed butt plug in my ass. He slowly twisted it, pulling it out one small section at a time. It was a plug made of three balls stacked together and a teardrop sphere on the tip. Each ball got bigger as they got closer to the base. I could feel my ass stretch and then tighten as each ball slipped out. When just the end was still inside me, he pushed forward, not stopping until the base was firmly pressed against my hole.

He started pulling it out again, then pushing it forward, back and forth. It felt wonderful, and my whimpers filled the entryway. Finally, I couldn't take it anymore. "Fuck me." I groaned. The pleasure from the plug was great, but I really wanted to feel him enter me. I could use the toy anytime but what I really wanted was his cock. "Fuck me." I said again, this time a little louder.

"I plan on it." He nipped my ass cheek again. "I just love watching your ass open and practically suck the plug back in. It's the hottest thing I've ever seen." I felt him reach forward and rub my balls. "God you have some big kiwis and kiwi has always been my favorite fruit. If I wasn't ready to explode, I'd take my time to see if yours taste as ripe as they feel." He said, as he finally removed the plug. As he stood up, I felt him slide his cock in the trench of my ass crack. I tried to thrust back against him but couldn't get much leverage without digging my chest and face into the wall.

"I'm going to uncuff you now." He said, stepping away from me, I presume to grab his key. "Only because you're going to need your hands to brace yourself against the wall." He returned and quickly removed the cuffs before tossing them aside. With my hands free, I reached behind my back and felt his abs, strong and covered in a moderate amount of hair. *So hot.* I moved my hands down his stomach, gliding through his pubic hair to wrap around his hard cock. I stroked him from the base to his moist head. He was thick and at least seven inches long, a good size bigger than the plug he'd just finished using to fuck me. I spread the moisture around his cock and stroked him a few times before planting my hands on the wall in front of me. I thrust my ass back into him making it clear what I wanted.

He rubbed his cock up and down my crack a few more times before stopping with the head against my opening. He slowly applied pressure, and I felt his cock forcing me to open wider to let him in. I relaxed and pushed back against him. He easily slipped inside, and it wasn't until he was about three quarters in that he was filling me deeper than the plug had. With his hands holding my hips, he took his time working his dick in further with short shallow thrusts, going a little deeper with each one. When he was fully sheathed inside my ass, he paused for a minute giving us both a chance to steady ourselves.

"Come on stud, fuck me like a mechanic." I said, letting him know I was ready.

"What?"

"Fuck me hard, the way you promised you would earlier." I begged him, needing his thick cock to pound into me mercilessly.

"Careful what you ask for." He warned.

I didn't have a chance to reply before he pulled his dick out and then swiftly thrust it back in. I moaned loudly. Fuck, his cock felt amazing filling me up. As he picked up his pace, he moved one hand to my shoulder for better control. He slid out until just the head was left encased within my ass, only to ram forward and pull out again. His strokes were long, powerful and they hit all of my pleasure buttons. It took most of my strength just to keep myself pushed away from the wall. He was grunting behind me as I kept up a continuous moan of encouragement.

His thrusts became erratic, and I knew he was getting close. I wanted to stroke myself off, but I needed both arms to keep myself braced against the wall. He thrust forward one final time and stayed buried deep inside me. He leaned forward covering my back with his chest. His teeth bit into my shoulder, going through my shirt. I grunted from the pressure, felt his body shudder as he shot his release. The hand that held my hip snaked around and grabbed my ready to explode cock. I looked down and watched him rub his thumb under my sensitive head before he started working his fist up and down my shaft. It took only a few strokes before I closed my eyes and felt myself erupting. When my body was done trembling, I opened my eyes to see I'd shot on his hand, as well as my t-shirt, but most had landed against the wall. I'd worry about cleaning up tomorrow.

I leaned my forehead against the wall to catch my breath, even though he'd done most of the work. "The police seem to like using excessive force in this city. I think I have wall burn on my chest." I said lethargically. "Not that I'm complaining."

"Sometimes, that's the only way to get the point across and teach a lesson." He said, as his softening cock slipped out of my ass.

"I'm not sure I learned my lesson, I may need another course. That was incredible." I said, finally breaking character. "See, I told you role playing would be fun."

"You weren't the one left standing on the side of the road like an idiot with a boner. I still can't believe you just yelled and drove off." He wiped his hand off on my shirt and then gave my ass another swat, leaving his hand where it landed.

"You really expected me to blow you through the car window, in broad daylight, and then drive home and masturbate to the memory?" I said in disbelief.

"That makes it more adventurous. No one would have noticed, and you love to jerk off!"

"I'd rather do it with you though. And as much as I love to blow you, the idea of then driving home and taking care of myself, just wasn't appealing."

"Fine, all future role playing will be planned with time and a location to allow for mutual release. It still wouldn't have killed you to blow me while I was on lunch."

"Role playing is meant to be sexy and spontaneous. My character was a compulsive liar with a rap sheet longer than Jersey. I had to get out of there. I even fibbed to Leia when I got home."

"What did you do to Princess Leia?"

"Nothing, we just talked. I told her I'd buy her a new toy if she helped me make sure her daddy wasn't pissed off at me by the change of plans."

"You better not have traumatized her; she's only eight months old. I thought I asked you not to speak in front of her when I'm not around to supervise."

"Relax she wouldn't do it, and I love her too. She could tell I was just in character and she mostly ignored me." A habit she had when I wasn't in character as well.

"Where is our poor dog now?"

"She's sleeping in her bed, I closed the door so she wouldn't disturb us. I also made sure she was very tired before you got home. We threw her ball for like three hours and she just wanted to keep going."

"Hope you didn't wear her out too much."

I needed to change the subject or we would end up debating whether I ruined the dog or not for the rest of the night, so I quickly changed the subject. "I didn't know you had a quota for handing out tickets."

"We don't, but part of our performance is evaluated by how many traffic citations we've handed out each month. Though, the guys will make wagers to see who can give out the most."

Leaning over, he gave me a quick kiss. "I'm going to go say hi to my other princess." I smiled at him as he walked away, not ready to move yet. "Love you."

I started counting in my head: *nineteen, twenty* — "Conrad!" Brayden yelled, right on cue, "You left the closet open, and the dog made a huge mess."

"Oops!" I yelled back. I had actually made a side deal with Leia – I would leave the closet open, and she could have anything she wanted that wasn't mine. In exchange, she would leave us alone while we got hot and sweaty. That way, if she woke up early, she wouldn't whine at the door. I loved her, but she was a total cock-block.

"It's not my stuff she's chewing on." He yelled back.

That bitch had double-crossed me. It's what I get for making a deal with a dog. Since I was well-fucked and completely satisfied at the moment, I couldn't find the energy to care. In that moment life was great.

THE END

I could feel the blood dripping down my face from the cut above my left eyebrow. A reminder I should have ended this match when I had the chance. Earlier I had quickly gotten the upper hand and had Striker pinned face down, my knee applying my full body weight into his lower back. Wrenching his arm back, I could have easily dislocated his shoulder or snapped his forearm. Would have been an easy win from there, but I have reservations about inflicting such damaging injuries just for a quick defeat.

I was regretting that now since Striker obviously didn't have those same hesitations. I managed to dodge a left hook aimed directly at my jaw. But ended up throwing my face into a strong right hand, connecting just above my left eye. I staggered back, unable to keep my balance, I tried to roll into the fall but the strike had left me dizzy. As I hit the mat, I slammed the left side of my face with the hard surface, splitting my cut open wider.

I didn't have much time to think about my injuries before Striker was straddling my back, trying to wrap his arm around my neck. I had my chin tucked against my chest preventing him from getting me in a rear naked choke. He tightened his arm on my chest, the pressure forcing the back of my head and neck against his upper body. Before he could get me into the choke, I put my palms flat on the mat and used what adrenaline I had left to push myself up onto my hands and knees.

Striker kept trying to get me in the hold, putting all his weight on my back. In an attempt to get him off me, I flipped us over. Trying to drive my weight into his stomach as we dropped onto the mat. I hoped the impact would force him to let go. We landed with him on his back, my back to his chest. Instead of letting go, he just constricted his arm tighter around my throat. I needed to make him loosen his grip, I could barely get a breath in at this point, I was scrambling. I frantically brought up my hands, digging my fingers firmly into his forearm. I pulled as hard as I could. He didn't budge. *Bastard.* Even though I couldn't move his arm, I was able to keep him from locking the choke in tighter. We both knew he was losing his grip, he couldn't hold the position much longer. That's when I felt Striker wrap his legs around my waist from behind. Crossing his ankles, he squeezed like his fucking life depended on it.

"Just give up, Cross." Striker grunted, his hot breath in my ear. I tried to shake my head 'no' as much as I could with his arm still squeezing tighter around my neck. He must be an idiot, he kept his face near my ear. I used the situation to my advantage by lifting my fist over my right shoulder and connecting squarely with the side of his right eye. He grunted and tightened his arm around my neck. I tried to get another swing to hit him again, but he moved his head out of my reach. I was already dizzy from the blow to my face and slamming my head against the mat earlier. Striker finally locked in the choke, within seconds began to see spots as he cut off the blood flow to my brain. Motherfucker was going to take me down.

I barely heard the crowd as they started cheering excitedly. I was always able to block out the crowd during a fight. Once every month, I came into The Cage to fight. I rarely lost, which is why those fickle fuckers watching loved it when it looked like I was losing. It was a small crowd, just a handful of guys with aggression issues they needed to release, but they could get loud. Staying focused was getting harder by the second. However, Striker knew me in The Cage, we had been here before. The only way I would submit, the only way to win against me was to beat me unconscious. Striker knew it well; he was one of only three guys from the group to have ever defeated me.

This was my twenty-sixth match, and fourth against Striker. I won two to one against him but it looked like we were about to be tied. I felt myself begin to slide into unconsciousness. My last thoughts were hoping I woke up without having lost too many brain cells, along with my pride.

****

When I slowly came to, my head was pounding. I felt like I was waking up from a punishing hangover, or more like three hangovers simultaneously wreaking havoc inside my head. I think I groaned a little but didn't open my eyes, just wanted to lay there until my head stopped spinning.

"It's about time you woke up," I heard a vaguely familiar voice say all too cheerfully. I scrunched my eyes tighter and grimaced. Striker must have noticed my reaction. "Sorry, man," he said a lot quieter and more soothing. "You know, losing wouldn't hurt so much if you just gave up before being put to sleep. We might be a bunch of assholes that like beating each other up, but none of us want to beat a man unconscious just to rack up a win."

I knew what he said made sense but I fought to win. Just giving up and admitting defeat wasn't satisfying. It was not my way. I had to fight until I couldn't open my eyes. That's why I worked hard to keep my body in great shape. I was quick on my feet, and had endurance to outlast almost everyone else I have come up against.

I'm 5'11" and 170 pounds of solid muscle. I run five miles every day to keep up my stamina, and I hit the gym four to five times a week. I have midnight black hair that I keep short on the sides and just long enough on top to style, but not long enough for an opponent to grab onto during a fight. I have strong facial features with a square jaw, high cheekbones and a sharp small nose. I've been lucky, even with all the fighting, I've never had my nose broken.

I was lying on the wrestling mat trying to breathe, but even small shallow breaths burned my throat like I had just done a round of battery acid shots. Even feeling this shitty, it was worth it to know I fought until I passed out. I don't quit. "Where's Buddy?" I managed to say without sounding too raspy. This was Buddy's group, his cellar which the guys called The Cage, was below his old farmhouse about 10 miles outside of Pittsburgh. Buddy was always here after the fights taking care of anyone that got hurt.

"Buddy had somewhere to be, I told him I would make sure you made it out of here and locked the place up when we left." He knew what I wanted to ask and answered before I could open my mouth, "Buddy made all the guys leave with him so they wouldn't be hovering. You were only out for twenty-three seconds but you know Buddy, he had the guys leaving before I even released the choke. Of course, I let go as soon as you lost consciousness, and it's not like you stopped breathing or anything. You're fine," he said as he grabbed my chin, manhandling me he pulled my head to the side, "except for this nasty cut above your eye. You'll have to work on those reflexes." I opened my eyes and glared, he was smirking.

Sexy fucking bastard. "Fuck you!" the croak in my voice made it sound less angry than I meant. I sounded like I was teasing, when I was about a minute away from breaking his smug nose.

"Maybe if you're a good boy," he said winking at me, conceited bastard. "Hold still, I'm going to clean it with some antiseptic."

He started scrubbing the pad on my open cut. I resisted the urge to flinch from the sting of the alcohol and how much pressure he was using. I felt like he was cleaning it with sandpaper. *Asshole!* Did he have to be so rough? I didn't want to seem like a baby but this was hurting worse than it did when I got the cut. "Your cut won't need stitches. Nothing seems broken, you'll probably just be light headed for a while and have a sore throat for a few hours. If you knew when to submit, it wouldn't bother you at all." He smirked again.

He said it like it would have been okay to tap out and just give up. I smiled, thinking next time I would break his arm and dislocate his shoulder if I got the chance. I felt Striker press a small bandage onto my cut, when he finished he said, "You can sit up now. But move slowly," Striker added as an afterthought like I haven't been choked out enough times to know not to move my head too fast. I gradually sat up and noticed my balance was fine, I was already feeling a lot less dizzy.

Striker pulled off his latex gloves and put them in a plastic trash can before reaching into his pack and grabbing a bottle of water and some pills. He turned back to me and asked, "Are you nauseous at all?" I thought about it for a second before slightly shaking my head. "Good. Sip a little of this," he said before opening the water and handing it to me. I took a cautious sip and was grateful when it soothed the burning in my throat. "Here, take four Ibuprofen, it will help with the swelling and you should feel better soon." I took the pills and swallowed them one at a time.

I looked closer at Striker's face, he was already starting to bruise around his right eye, it would be a nice shiner in a few hours. He deserved it, just for being a smug bastard. He was about two inches taller than me but his body was the same compact build as mine. He wore his dark brown hair in the same style as me. His face was softer and more round. I had a rougher look, which some might even call ruggedly handsome, but Striker he was just stunningly beautiful. Just when my eyes were starting to take a full appreciative look of his body, he turned his head and locked his gaze onto mine.

Not wanting to be caught admiring him, I narrowed my eyes and glared. Half smiling, he scowled back at me. We were only about a foot apart, and I couldn't tell if he wanted to hit me or kiss me. I wasn't friends with any of the guys I fought against, I didn't talk to them outside of arranging fights so I knew nothing about any of them. This was the longest conversation I'd ever had with Striker and I had only really said a few words. He was gorgeous, and if I had met him anywhere else I would have taken him home and fucked him. But I don't make a habit of sleeping with guys and then beating the shit out of them.

"When are we having a rematch?" I asked. My voice sounded raspier than usual and my throat still burned when I spoke.

Striker shook his head. "There won't be a rematch. This was my last fight, I'm getting too old to keep making excuses for why I have bruises and tired of people assuming I'm always starting fights. I used to really love fighting and it was great for releasing tension but I'm ready to find a new release that doesn't leave bruises and broken bones."

"What the fuck? That can't be your last fight; you have to give me a rematch. We have a two-two tie, you can't let it end like that," I said raising my voice as loud as I could, ignoring my sore throat.

"I told Buddy before the fight this would be my last one. I don't see the problem ending with a tie. Equal!" he snapped back.

"It's unsportsmanlike to refuse the looser a rematch. Stop being such a pussy," I said probably sounding childish, but I wanted my rematch. I had to win our last fight, I had to be at the top.

He looked thoughtful for a minute, grinning at me slyly, "I thought you might say something like that so I will give you a rematch but I have a few stipulations."

"And those would be what?" I asked irritably, he sounded like a diva. "You need your own pansy-ass dressing room?"

"I was thinking it would be at my house, no audience, and just grappling. That way you won't be as embarrassed when I make you my bitch."

It was on the tip of my tongue to say no because I liked striking, and wanted to give him matching black eyes, but I'm very competitive and I wanted a rematch. And although I preferred fighting with my fists, grappling could be a good release of tension. "When are we going to do this?"

He gave me a playful grin before responding, "Tonight, if you're up for it, that is." Even if I wasn't feeling up to it, I wouldn't have been able to refuse the challenge in his statement. I just nodded my head. "If you think you're okay to drive, you can just follow me home or you can ride with me if you want," Striker said as he pulled sweats on over his athletic shorts. I got up and went to do the same.

Finished putting my clothes and shoes on, I turned around to see Striker watching me from the bottom of the stairs, his bag thrown over his shoulder. I grabbed my bag and went over to him. He motioned me to go up first. I waited by our cars while he shut off the lights and locked the doors.

"I live about 30 minutes from here, if you're sure you can drive, and are up for another fight," Striker said as he approached the cars.

"I'm fine," I grunted. "Let's go."

****

"Are you sure you don't want to shower first?" Striker asked for the second time since arriving at his house a few minutes ago. I shook my head, like I did when he offered a drink or asked if I wanted to relax on his couch.

"I just want to get to the grappling. Why shower when we will just be getting sweaty again?" I asked irritably.

"Okay, have it your way," he said with another smirk before sauntering into his room. A few minutes later, he came out in just a bright red jockstrap. There's no way he could have fought earlier in this jock, with how little support it provided. His cock and balls were barely contained in that small front pouch. The jock was only held up by the thin waist strap, which was barely above the base of his cock, a couple inches below his waist. Then an even thinner strap from the base of the fabric below Striker's balls looped around each thigh just below his firm, round ass. "My shorts are in the dryer downstairs. Follow me." Walking down the stairs after him, I couldn't keep my eyes off his ass.

The basement was where he had his laundry supplies in one corner, the rest of the room was a home gym, he also had a large mat in the back corner. I walked over to the mat, standing there in just my black shorts, I watched as Striker ruffled around with the clothes in the dryer. After finding the pair of shorts he wanted, he leisurely bent over and stepped into them. He slowly pulled them up his legs, flexing his ass as he stood. I had to hold in a moan at the view he was giving me. By the time he finished his reverse-strip tease, I was uncomfortably hard in my own jock.

Now we were getting into position to start our rematch. He was standing on the mat across from me in nothing but his tight white shorts. Tight enough I could see his skimpy red jock through them. I was having trouble concentrating since I couldn't make myself look anywhere but at Striker's barely covered cock. Striker asked if I was ready, I absently nodded my head. I was expecting us to circle around each other, waiting for an opening to make a move but as soon as I nodded Striker was on me. He skipped the clinch and just slid around to my back, quickly locking his arms around my midsection. He then pulled my back tight against his chest, pinning my arms to my sides.

"You're gonna have to be faster than that if you want to win, baby, and trust me you want to win. Winner gets a very special prize," he whispered in my ear as he ground his hardening cock into my ass.

"You're cheating." I whined like a little bitch before I could stop myself. If my hands had been free I would have introduced my palm to the side of his face.

Striker just chuckled before whispering in my ear again, "It's not cheating, I'm just using your attraction to me to my tactical advantage." I knew he was right, I wanted him so bad I wasn't even trying to escape his hold. "Winner gets to top, and after I win I am going to ride you so hard you won't walk right for a week."

He was blatantly cheating, even though I could easily break his hold I didn't want to, I was enjoying the feeling of his body caressing mine and how his light breathing against my neck made my body tingle. I was lost in how easily his stiff cock just pushed my ass cheeks apart, snuggling and rubbing between them like it belonged there. Even through the jock and shorts, I could feel every hard inch. I got lost in the pleasure of him rubbing against me for a moment, but then I started thinking about his tight ass bending over and all I wanted was to pound my cock into his ass. I liked that idea; I had to win and then I was going to fuck him until he passed out.

"If you're not even going to try, I might as well tie you to my workout bench with my hand wraps and spend the rest of the night fucking your ass." He paused to lightly bite my neck where it curved into my shoulder. I think I moaned or whimpered or made some sound I normally wouldn't make. "I was hoping for a challenge before I claimed your ass. You want to just bend over for me instead?"

"You know, you're an asshole," I grunted out as I lightly tested his hold to see how easily I could slip out of it. If he thought I'd just submit because I liked how his cock nestled against my ass, he had a surprise coming.

"You'll be a complete slut for me, you'll be begging me to fuck you. I've been waiting to fuck you into submission since I first watched you fight. You don't know how many times I've jerked off thinking about tying you to my bed and fucking you senseless," Striker practically growled in my ear.

I almost let myself whimper, "Please," but caught myself in time. No matter how much Striker made me want him, I wouldn't let him have the satisfaction of dominating me. He was already an egotistical prick, and I'm sure he would find a way to rub my nose in it if I lost, or worse if I did just roll over with my ass in the air for him.

With renewed determination, I was thinking through my best options to quickly end the match. He kept rambling about all the dirty things he could do to my ass, and how I'd beg him for more. Then he surprised me when he jerked me harder against his chest, bringing my feet a couple inches off the ground before he twisted and slammed us both onto the mat. The impact against my stomach knocked the air out of me. Striker was still on my back, but his arms were no longer wrapped around me.

I managed to flip onto my back, making our chests touch. I lifted my legs and crossed them over Striker's waist. I was hoping that by getting him into full guard it would help me flip him, but instead it just made our cocks rub against each other through our shorts and jocks. Striker had his face hovering above mine, and as he rubbed his crotch against mine, he leaned down and kissed me.

Oh, sweet baby Jesus, his lips were perfect as they covered mine. I moaned and he thrust his tongue into my mouth. I was lost in his kiss and the feeling of his hard cock grinding against my own, fuck he was going to make me cream in my shorts. It was a few minutes before I got my head back in the game. Once again, I was reminding myself we were fighting and that I was going to win that fight. I pushed at his shoulders and he pulled back licking his lips.

"You cheating fuckface, that has to be a disqualification, foreign objects aren't allowed. And that tongue is definitely a foreign object."

Striker just grinned at me before responding, "Really? You want to win by a disqualification?" Fuck, when he put it like that it did make me sound like a chicken-shit.

"No, I would much rather kick your ass," I said before sweeping out from under Striker and rolling him into a mount, he ended up on his back with me straddling his hips. I was stretched out over him holding his biceps to the mat. Instead of trying to break my grip or reverse our positions, he began thrusting his hard cock against my ass. He pulled both his legs up with his feet flat on the ground making his thrusts sturdier. Bouncing me a little each time he shoved up against me. Bastard.

I was so turned on I could barely focus at all and he just licked his lips. "If you wanted to ride me, all you had to do was say so," he purred, trying to sound seductive. Sexy fucker thought he was just so smooth, and I'm sure with his devilish smile and sly tongue most guys ate it up, or dropped to their knees and sucked it up. I waited for him to thrust his hips up and I pushed myself forward so I could get my knees on his shoulders. As I did that, I reached behind me with my right arm and hooked it around his thigh under his knee. I watched the smirk fade from his face as he realized I was about to pin him. He tried to struggle, but I already had his leg in a firm grip, and my knees were pressing his shoulders into the mat.

He gave up struggling after a few seconds and just looked at me. "Guess you win. Better go grab the lube and condoms above the dryer before you claim your prize." I just nodded before getting up and walking across the room to get the supplies. When I turned back around, Striker was on his knees with his face on the mat, his ass in the air. He had removed his white shorts but remained in his jock. His knees were far enough apart I could see my prize. I wanted to rush over and dive into that sweet ass, but made myself go slowly. I wanted Striker to think I was in control even though I knew if he ordered me to do something, I'd do whatever the hell he wanted.

Kneeling behind him, I put my hands on his firm ass cheeks and started squeezing. Like a target, the jocks waistband and the straps around each thigh framed his ass perfectly, leaving his hole in the center waiting to be fucked. I leaned in with my mouth open and gently nipped at his left cheek. He moaned and I bit his other cheek but much harder, just let my teeth sink in, not hard enough to break the skin, just hard enough to leave my mark. I loved the taste of his skin, salty from sweating but it was a clean manly sweat. It even smelled delicious. I used my tongue and slowly licked my way up to his lower back.

"Please," Striker moaned, "fuck me already."

"You know for as enthusiastic as you were to fuck me, you sure are an eager bottom."

"I'm just a horny bastard. I love to drive, but I am just as happy to go along for the ride." He wiggled his sexy ass at me again. "Shut up and get to fucking."

"No," I said firmly, "I will decide when or if I fuck you." I wasn't sure when I got myself back under control, but I was planning to keep it that way. "Suck me," I ordered as I stood back up. I was pleased when Striker immediately pushed himself up onto his knees. He turned to face me and quickly pulled my shorts down around my ankles, leaving me in my black jockstrap. Leaning forward, he put his mouth over the head of my covered cock. He continued sucking my hard cock through my jock while he glided his hands over the back of my legs working his way up until he was cupping my ass.

I let out a gasp when he gripped my ass hard and pulled my crotch tight to his face as he moved his lips from the head of my cock down the shaft. He was wild and uninhibited, he knew what he was doing and loving every second. When he started sucking my balls through my jock, my knees almost gave out, it was too much. I put my hand on the side of his head, and pulled him off. He looked up at me and cocked his head a little to the side. I could tell he wanted to know why I stopped him.

"I said suck me, not tease me." I pulled down the waistband of my jock, hooking it below my balls and pushing them forward. I grabbed my dick by the base and pointed it at Striker's eager mouth. "Now suck it while I decide if I'm going to come down your throat or up your ass."

Striker leaned forward and inhaled my cock, taking it all the way in until his lips met my fingers. I moved my hand and he swallowed the remaining couple of inches. His chin pushed my balls back against my jock, the pressure on my balls felt amazing. He rubbed his nose in my pubic hair before looking up at me. He slowly pulled my cock out of his mouth before swallowing it whole again. He closed his eyes and started sucking up and down; Striker sucked cock like he was suffocating and his only source of oxygen was in my balls.

He didn't just suck my dick, he worshiped it. Using his tongue, he teased the underside of the head before pressing it against my slit. I could only whimper, his tongue drove me so crazy. Then he deep throated me again and pressed his teeth lightly against the base of my cock with just enough pressure to feel incredible. The stimulation was too much, he was going to make me come too soon.

He had only been sucking me for a few minutes when I used my hand on his head to make him stop again. "Put your face back down on the mat so I can fuck you." He quickly turned around and dropped his upper-body to the mat, leaving his ass in the air. I kicked my shorts off before removing my jock and tossing it behind me. Reaching down I picked up the condom from where I dropped it earlier. I quickly opened it and rolled it down my spit-slicked cock. I grabbed the lube off the mat and squeezed some onto the top of his crack. His legs were spread out enough I could watch it drip down his ass, mixing with the sweat that was already there. I used my finger to rub it around his hole before pushing into him.

"No, just lube your cock and fuck me!" Striker ordered. I thought about continuing to stretch him but I wanted to fuck him the way he wanted, and his tone made it clear he wanted it rough. I poured more lube around his crease before generously slicking my cock. I lined up my cock and slowly started to push in. I had the head just past the rim when Striker growled and pushed himself back, only stopping when his ass hit my thighs and my entire length was deep inside him. I moaned at the feeling of being completely surrounded by him. "Don't move until I tell you. I need a second to adjust."

I rubbed my hand over the bite mark I left on his ass while I waited for him to get comfortable. He looked fucking hot wearing my mark, I'd be sure to give him a few more. A few moments later Striker panted. "Okay, fuck me like you paid for it." I think I might have suffered some brain damage earlier because I didn't know what he meant.

"What the fuck does that mean?"

"Fuck me like you would a whore. Hard, fast, dirty, but don't cry after," he snapped back at me. I didn't have a problem fucking him rough and dirty. Tired of waiting for me, he started rocking back and forth on my cock. Taking charge, I clamped my hands on his hips to hold him still. I pulled my cock slowly out of his ass, he whimpered when the head of my cock was out completely but didn't say anything. Good. I was tired of him trying to top from the bottom. Without warning I thrust back into him with all the force I could generate. We both moaned and grunted as I kept pulling out and pushing back in, making it rough like he wanted.

I pounded his ass vigorously, fucking him as hard as I could and he still moaned and begged for more. It felt amazing and I knew I wouldn't be able to keep it up for long. I had needed to come since I followed him down the stairs earlier. I was so lost in my own pleasure I wasn't even listening to Striker, but I'm sure he was talking dirty when he wasn't moaning. I started shortening my thrusts so I could lean down against Striker's back. I slid my hands from his waist up to his nipples, pinching them as I bit his shoulder, not hard enough to break the skin but hard enough it smarted.

He lifted his head off the mat and turned towards me. "Yeah, baby, punish me for teasing you so bad." I twisted his nipples hard as I continued to thrust forcefully. I stopped leaving marks on his shoulder and turned my head to cover his lips with mine. I kissed him hard and fucked his mouth with my tongue with the same enthusiasm I was pounding his ass.

He pulled his mouth away before shouting, "Oh shit, Cross. I'm coming." I felt his body tense under me and his ass tightened around my cock. I leaned back up, grabbed the thigh straps of his jock, and pulled them tight knowing it would put pressure on his balls and cock. I used them as handles while I fucked him through his orgasm. He started moaning, "Oh fuck, oh God." When I was about ready to come, I pulled out of him and removed the condom before erupting all over his back. He did say he wanted me to fuck him like a whore.

"That how you like it, bitch?" I couldn't help taunting as he collapsed on his stomach. I fell to my side next to him.

He looked at me and smiled. "That's how I love it, you made me come in my jockstrap."

"You like it dirty," I teased.

"You didn't even touch my dick." I didn't know how to respond to that so I just smiled that I made him come just from fucking him.

We laid there for a few minutes before I asked, "You let me win, didn't you?"

He chuckled lightly before leaning over and giving me a quick kiss. "Depends on your perspective. To me I'm definitely the winner here, besides this was just round one," he winked before leaning in and kissing me, he was ready to start round two.

THE END

Dirty Zero
Copyright© 2012 Kyle Adams

"'Lo, Wyatt!" someone yelled waving their hand in front of my face, blocking my comic book. Didn't they know it was rude to interrupt someone while they were reading? Especially since Captain Uptightedness was just about to plunder Daring Audacity's secret cavern. This was the final issue before starting the next story arc. It just came out today and I had spent half my lunch break driving to the comic book store. I had to know how this arc ended. Things really picked up four issues ago when Audacity killed TemTitus, Captain Uptightedness's young protégé. The last issue had ended with the Captain not only learning the location of the Audacity Lair, but also that his arch-nemesis Audacity was really his dead younger brother, well, not so dead. And now, because of some Jackass interrupting me, I wasn't going to be able to finish before I had to go back to work. I knew I should have read in my car but the couch in the break room is so comfortable. Usually, there is no one around on my break since I take it an hour later than everyone else.

"What," I grunted not bothering to look up from my comic. Using my hand, I motioned for the jerk to move theirs. I would have shoved it out of my face but my hand sanitizer was at my desk and I had no idea where this hand had been. Soon as the jerk's hand moved, I'd be able to finish my story.

"Sorry, Wyatt, didn't mean to put my hand in your face but didn't know how else to get your attention. I said your name like eight times and you never answered." Oh, man, I knew that deep sultry voice belonged to Brian, the super-hot, nice, and totally out of my league office heartthrob. I tilted my head and slowly peeked up, the deepest green eyes I have ever seen were looking back at me.

Why was Brian even talking to me? Didn't he know I couldn't function around him? He was tall and handsome, with his muscular body and chiseled face. Simply put he was hot, hotter than any character from my comic books. I get nervous enough around normal people but when Brian is near, I turn into a complete ass. I just stare at him without blinking like a total freak, and you can forget talking, my mouth just quits working. I fought the urge to push my glasses up, I am sure he already thought I was a stupid loser, I've never been able to say a full sentence around him. Usually, I would just answer his questions by shaking my head. I wasn't much better at talking to other people but at least with them I could usually say a full sentence.

"W-What?" I repeated more hesitantly, proud I only stuttered once. Hoping a one word answer counted as a full sentence.

Brian smiled his trademark smile that always made my cock hard and my knees soft. Luckily, I was sitting and the comic covered my crotch so I didn't have to try to hide my erection this time. "I asked you to come to my house next Friday night. My sister is using my place to have a party and I want you to come." I was about to shake my head, like I always do when he invites me out for drinks, bowling or whatever the guys were doing. "It's a superhero party, you have to come. There's a prize for best costume."

Instead of shaking my head, I just stared up at him, my mouth open. Was he serious? "Come on, you have a week and a half to get ready. You can even wear a mask, hide your identity if you want," he probably thought I'd be more comfortable if no one knew who I was. Ha! Poor Brian, little did he know that nothing makes me comfortable in social situations.

"I-I'll consider the o-option," I stammered. Breaking away from his mesmerizing eyes, I managed to look back at my comic. I figured I should make the effort and go, it's not like it would hurt to get out there and try to meet people. I was twenty-five, and couldn't remember the last time I had sex. Was it in college? Yeah, it was probably time to start putting myself out there, as scary as that thought was.

"Hey," he said grabbing my chin and tilting my face up. He slid his hand up my cheek, and adjusted my glasses before brushing my hair behind my ear. He rested his hand there, rubbing little circles on my cheek with his thumb. Luckily I was so stunned into silence that I just sat there, without moving and didn't start panting like a dog in heat. "You'll have fun, I promise." I wasn't sure if it was my imagination but I think his voice sounded huskier than usual. There seemed to be a lot of innuendo behind that statement. He removed his hand and whispered, "Please come," and I almost did, right in my pants. Without waiting for me to react, he straightened and headed for the door. I watched as he left the break room, happy as can be, while I sat there with an aching cock, a forgotten comic, and dirty fantasies I didn't think could possibly come true.

What was all that low talking and hand on my face about? Was he gay? Did he like me? Yeah right! Even if he was gay, he wouldn't want a skinny nerd like me. There was no way Brian actually wanted me 'like that'. With that happy thought, I stood up to get back to my office. As soon as I looked down, I realized I had a raging hard on. Apparently, the memo that Brian was not into me never got to my cock. Awesome. Now I'd have to slip into the bathroom and rub one out before I could get back to work.

****

The next Friday, I found myself standing at Brian's front door dressed as Moltenman. My costume was high-end and matched the comic's exactly. Moltenman wasn't my favorite hero, hell he was really a sidekick, but he was the only character I liked who had a scrawny body like mine. Of course, he didn't need a big body when he could control water, turning it to solid ice instantly, or heating it so it was hotter than lava. And he could fly. Actually, the physics of it made no sense, even by comic standards, but the outfit was cool.

In the light it was black with deep blue waves running up my legs and across my midsection. In the dark, the blue waves glowed and flickered, looking more like flames with orange hues. Trust me, it's an awesome costume. The mask had the same color theme, but only covered a thin strip of my face around my eyes. I had to wear my contacts with the mask. I didn't wear contacts very often, so my left eye kept twitching and getting a bit irritated. Great, my eye would probably get all red and I'd look like I had pink eye or something.

I rang the bell before someone driving by crashed because they were staring at the freak dressed up like a superhero lurking outside a nice house in a ritzy neighborhood. I rang the bell, twice. All of a sudden I feared someone would shoot the crazy first, ask questions later.

The door opened, revealing a helpless looking young woman, she was smiling warmly at me, unaware of all the potential dangers around. Simpleton. Not very creative either, her outfit was just low-rise jeans and a low-cut tank top. Typical tramp in distress.

Her smile faded. "Excuse me, did you just call me a typical tramp?" Oh god, did I say that out loud? Being socially retarded sucked. I either get tongue tied or forget how to think quietly.

"U-um n-no I meat, meant..." Idiot, I told myself, be Moltenman. "I said tropical amp. You know, like electric, 'cause you look so alive." I gave her a stern look, so she'd know I meant business. I mentally sighed when she smiled again, I can't believe she bought that.

"Oh, I do, don't I? You must be Wyatt, Brain said you were cute but he didn't say you were so sweet. I'm his sister, Olivia," she said holding her hand out; I gripped it firmly and shook it twice. "Please, come in we're just wrapping up in the living room," she stopped to giggle a little. "I mean the party is just getting started, in the living room, head on in."

I admit I haven't been to a lot of parties before so I don't have much to compare with but walking into the living room I was pretty sure this wasn't a party. It certainly wasn't a costume party, unless they were all dressed as sluttier than average innocent civilians. There were about 12 to 15 women sitting in a semicircle. They were all facing towards the front of the room, where a woman was standing. She was holding up a giant double headed purple dildo, looking closer I could see a table behind her lined with sex toys. My left eye twitched a few times. Brian tricked me into dressing up and coming to a Pleasure Party. The ladies noticed my entrance; the woman in the center stopped talking and just stared at me. Like in slow motion, they all turned to me one at a time, all looking at me curiously while I looked around the room, wondering if it was too late to escape.

One woman finally broke the silence, "Holy Shit! I didn't know you got a stripper for this!" She used her hands to gesture me towards the center of the room. I didn't move. "Come on, sweet-thing, start dancing." By this time the other ladies had joined in and where chanting 'take it off' and 'shake that ass'. Why the fuck did Brian invite me here? I was mortified and even my Moltenman persona abandoned me. Shit, I had to get out of here.

I didn't want to take my eyes off them, they were starting to get more rowdy and I was worried if I turned my back they'd swarm me. If that pack of crazy bitches took me down, I wouldn't be getting back up. Not even Moltenman had the survival skills for something like this. Hoping to escape, I took a step back and bumped into something solid. There was nothing there when I came in, so it had to be person. It felt too flat, solid and big to be a woman. I gulped, not sure, if I should try to spin away and dash for the door.

I never got a chance to do either because, before I could make a move, something was slipped over my head, and strong arms wrapped around my upper body pulling me tighter against the mystery man's chest. I couldn't see or move my arms. I struggled to get free and started screaming, I was probably another minute away from completely panicking.

Then I heard, "It's me," whispered quietly in my ear. I stopped struggling, realizing it was Brian holding me, and I immediately felt safe knowing I was under his control. "That's right, Moltenman, struggling is useless. You walked right into my trap, now I'll take you to my torture chamber and you'll tell me the location of the Gold Griffin Gemstone, by the time I'm through with you," he said in a deep throaty voice followed by a menacing laugh.

He spun me around so fast I got dizzy and before I knew it, something was pulled tight round me and I still couldn't move my arms. Next, my ankles were tied together. I almost fell over when the rope was pulled snug but a large hand on my chest kept me steady. I felt Brian press against my waist as his arms enclosed around me before he lifted me over his shoulder.

I wiggled as the position put pressure on my rapidly hardening cock. "Don't move," he ordered in his villainous voice. My body stopped moving on its own but my cock continued to harden to a full erection. He was even stronger than I thought and could carry me with ease.

I felt Brian start to walk away when one of the ladies shouted, "Where the hell do you think you're going? We wanna watch." These women are perverts, don't they have internet? Brian's incredibly hot though so I understood wanting to watch him.

"Sorry to disappoint but I'm a villain and can't share my torture techniques," Brian moved his hand to cover my ass as he was speaking. He was really getting into this superhero play and I wasn't complaining. I loved how his hand felt kneading my butt.

"Okay girls, let's wrap this up so we can get out of here before the screaming starts," I heard Olivia say as Brian started walking again.

"I want to stay for the screaming," I heard one woman say before another said, "I hope they at least record it." All noises stopped when I heard Brian close a door before he started walking down stairs, or that's what it felt like. A few minutes later, I felt Brian drop me. Before I could worry about falling, I landed with a bounce on something soft. A bed, I thought. Brian quickly adjusted me so I was lying on my back.

He untied the ropes around my upper body but left my legs bound. I felt him pull my top up, exposing my stomach. He kept pulling until my arms slipped free but didn't pull the shirt over my head. He didn't want me to see yet. I thought about using my now freed arms to try and get away but I knew Brian wouldn't hurt me and I wanted to see what he was up to. He rubbed his hands over my stomach and chest, lightly touching me. The bed started moving a little before I felt him swing his leg over my stomach, so that he was straddling my chest.

Slowly, he moved both hands up my right arm until he got to the wrist. He caressed it a couple times before I felt smooth silk wrapping around my wrist. He tied the other end of the silk to something. When he let go of my wrist, I tugged a few times but the hold was completely secure.

He did the same with my left arm, being just as gentle. "These restraints are made out of Regamite, your only known power inhibitor, now you're completely at my mercy," Brian informed me before he removed the bag from over my head, it was a black pillow-case. Then he finished taking my shirt off, tossing it to the floor.

I found myself staring up into Brian's green eyes. He was wearing a huge smirk and I'd never seen him look so pleased. He wore a black eye mask with one blue-silver diamond embedded under his left eye, positioned where a tear would fall. He was wearing a skintight black body suit, larger versions of the same teardrop diamonds ran up both

- 53 -

arms, all the way to form a circle around his collar. Over his heart, bare skin showed through where a diamond shape of fabric was cut out. Both his fists were covered in black leather, layers of diamond-tears were embedded in the back of the gloves. Brian was wearing a Darkfist costume and he pulled off the look perfectly. I had to bite my bottom lip to keep from moaning.

Darkfist is the hottest of all the villains. It's been said Darkfist cried tears of diamonds but vowed the teardrop on his mask would be the last diamond-tear he shed. He would never again care about anything or anyone enough to cry for it. According to legend, after witnessing the brutal slaughter of everyone he loved, he cried diamond-tears for four days. Each tear was a piece of his humanity and he only stopped mourning after the last drop fell. He made his suit with a portion of the diamonds and hid the rest. Some say the diamonds actually provide him with his inhuman strength and seemingly endless supply of energy. It's thought that if someone found the diamonds, they would be Darkfist's one weakness.

Looking up at Brian and his devilish smirk it was obvious he didn't have the same dark past but he still looked hot in the Darkfist uniform. Looking down at me, he brought his gloved hand to my cheek. Gently, he rubbed his thumb along my bottom lip before moving his hand to the back of my head. He lifted my head, putting a pillow under it before pulling his hand away. I winced as some strands of my shaggy hair got caught in his gloves.

"Sorry," he whispered, "I'll take the gloves off, better for touching you that way." I watched as he removed the gloves and tossed them aside. Looking around the room for the first time I noticed it was very dark with only a small light above the bed. The walls must be black because I couldn't even make out where they were. Beside the bed was a black rhombus-shaped nightstand. The dark room was very fitting for Darkfist. I looked over where my wrist was tied to the headboard; it had bars crossing each other, making rows of diamonds. Brian really went all out for this.

I felt him untying the rope around my legs; I didn't even notice he had moved. After it was removed, he gently rubbed each leg. It felt too nice to tell him it was unnecessary, the rope was loose enough not to cut off circulation or anything.

Crawling back over me, he smiled deviously, making me quiver. He kept moving until his face was above mine. "I need to stop playing for a minute. I have to kiss you now." He leaned down and gently pressed his lips to mine. All I could do was whimper and follow his lead. I felt his tongue rub against my lips, I opened my mouth and he pushed his tongue in, brushing it against mine. He kept supporting his weight on one arm while he put the other behind my head, running his fingers through my curls. He grabbed my hair and pulled me tighter against his lips, allowing his tongue to invade my mouth even further.

Gripping my hair tighter, he pulled my head back and rested our foreheads together. "I need a minute before getting back into character," he breathed softly against my lips. "And I need to ask you a personal question, is that okay?" I nodded. He sighed, "Are you still a virgin? Don't be embarrassed, it'd actually be really hot if you were, but I just need to know how far I can take the playing."

"N-not a virgin," I answered, leaving out that I've only been with two people before and had only had sex a whopping five times. He only asked if I was a virgin and I was lucky I managed to say as much as I did with his lips right there in front of me.

"Have you ever been tied up before?" I shook my head. "If you want me to stop anything or to untie you just tell me and I will, understand?" I nodded. "Good." He leaned down and pressed his lips to mine again. He pulled away and gave me another sly grin.

He sat up so his ass rested on top of my hard cock. "You have something I want, Moltenman, and I'm willing to do anything it takes to get it." He rubbed back and forth on my cock, obviously teasing me. "Have you ever heard of sexual torture Moltenman?" I shook my head. "When you're as bad as me, you learn the most efficient methods to get what you want." He brought his index finger up to his mouth and slowly licked the tip before sucking his whole finger into his mouth. He brought his wet finger down to my chest and started slowly rubbing my nipple. I whimpered, my back arched, and my arms pulled against the restraints but they held tight.

"I'm going to slowly get you worked up, you'll be needing to release so hard but you won't be able to until I let you. You'll be so desperate and needy to come, you'll spill all your secrets to me, praying I'll let you come," he taunted me. He had to feel my hard cock against his ass, and know I was already needy, and willing to tell him anything.

He got up and moved over so he could start pulling off my tights. He moved so slow and seemed to be trying to memorize every new patch of skin that he uncovered. When he finished, he just stood there looking at me. I felt embarrassed and wondered if he was disgusted by what he saw, would he just leave me tied there?

"Jesus, Wyatt, I knew you were beautiful but had no idea you'd be this hot," he said then frowned slightly. "I mean, Moltenman, I should have figured you'd have a tight swimmers build, controlling water and all but damn, I wasn't expecting such perfection. I'll enjoy tormenting you immensely." I think I was more embarrassed by his over-the-top compliments than I was from having him see me naked. Still, I was tied down, he wasn't repulsed, and I was anxious to see where this was going.

He walked over to the nightstand and opened a drawer. I couldn't see what was in it but he made an "aha" sound before turning around. "Time to put you in the first torture device," he smiled, crawling between my legs, not letting me see what he had grabbed. He adjusted them so my feet rested flat on the bed with my bent knees spread apart. Brian was lying flat on his stomach with his face right in front of my balls. He looked up at me, an even bigger grin on his face. "I have to prepare the torture area first." I watched more than felt the first swipe of his tongue against my balls. When he pressed his tongue firmly against them, I had to fight the urge to thrust into the air. I groaned as he wrapped his lips around one testicle and sucked it into his mouth. He used his tongue to rub and gently poke against it. I was moaning loudly but Brian didn't seem to notice as he switched his attentions to my other testicle, giving it the same slow, torturous attention.

Moving his attention up, he licked all the way to the tip of my cock. He swiped the precome that gathered there before he gently pressed his tongue against the slit. He continued to tease me and it felt good but not enough to give me what I needed. Finally, he took the whole head in his mouth, then let it slip back out. I groaned wanting more. "So needy already and I'm just getting started. You have a beautiful cock and it tastes so good." That I was willing to believe, on my small 5'8" frame, my thick seven inches looked impressive.

He turned his attention back to my cock and swallowed it whole. I reflexively bucked up into his throat, letting out a gasp at the wonderful surprise. He grabbed my hips and pushed them down, clearly indicating he was in control. Damn, his mouth was amazing. He slid his lips up and down; making sure his tongue was always in on the action. After a few too short minutes, he pulled off. He wiped the back of his hand across his mouth before grinning at me. "I can keep this up for hours but it looks like you're ready to come already. Don't worry, I won't let you," he said holding up a small adjustable, leather cock ring. So that's what he got out of the drawer.

He wrapped the ring around the base of my cock, snapping the buttons together. Then wrapped the other part around my ball sac right where it hung down from my body. With the ring secured, he started sucking me again while fondling my balls with his hand. His other hand crept up my stomach until it reached my nipple. He rubbed and squeezed it gently.

It was too much and my body was desperate for release, I wasn't used to delayed gratification. I was whimpering and begging him to let me come, but he just kept his attention on further exciting me. When he pulled up, I looked at him pleadingly and whimpered a "please" or hoped I did. Working his way up my body, he stopped to lick my nipples. When he reached my face he leaned close, his green eyes gazed into mine, he whispered, "So beautiful," before closing his eyes and pressing his lips firmly against mine. It wasn't a slow tender kiss like earlier, this was a passionate, hard kiss. He wanted me as much as I wanted him. He grabbed my hair again, and pulled me away "I think it's time to move onto the next level."

He went back to the nightstand but this time he didn't hide what he grabbed. In one hand, he had a bottle of lube and the other was a smooth glass dildo. Kneeling between my legs, he set the lube and dildo beside my hip. He reached over and got a pillow, lifting my legs and raising my ass off the mattress, he put the pillow under my lower back. He kept one of my legs in the air and lowered the other back to the bed before he picked up the lube.

I watched as he poured it on his fingers, warming it between them before he started rubbing over my hole. He was watching my face, making sure I was okay with what he was doing. "Please," I begged softly. I knew he got the message when he slowly inserted one finger into my ass. His finger inside me felt good but not exactly what I really wanted or needed. I may not have had much sex with another person but that didn't mean I didn't have a diverse toy collection. Using just the one finger, he continued to loosen me up for a few minutes, before sliding another finger in. He kept switching his gaze from my face to watch his fingers pushing in and out of me.

Minutes later, he removed his fingers and lowered my other leg back to the bed. I whimpered in protest, wanting him to keep going. "I'm not done with your ass," was all he said before he picked up the dildo. It looked about six inches long and only a bit thicker than one of Brian's fingers. After lubing the dildo, he rubbed it over my hole a few times before slowly pushing into me. He teased me, inserting the tip before quickly removing it. Doing that a couple times, he surprised me when he forced it all the way inside with one quick shove. He left it pushed in while he leaned down and started licking and sucking on my balls again.

He was driving me crazy with too much stimulation and yet it still wasn't enough. He moved his mouth back to my cock and started sucking while he played with the dildo. He pulled it almost all the way out. I arched my back and cried out when he shoved two fingers in alongside the dildo. He set a fast pace, pushing in and out of my ass with strong, even thrusts.

After a few minutes, with his hot mouth working my cock while his fingers and dildo filled my ass, he had me ready to come, even with the cock ring on. "Fuck, don't stop!" I wished I could take back my outburst when he removed his mouth from my cock and stopped thrusting into me.

Looking up, he grinned. "You can't come yet, you still haven't sung like a canary." I was on the edge of release and had no clue why he was talking about birds. I looked at him with my pleading blue eyes. Hoping he'd take pity and finish me off. He just shook his head.

What the hell? He was hot but it's unfortunate he can't seem to differentiate between sex and a fucking inquisition. Oh shit, judging by his smirk falling into a scowl I was willing to bet I just thought that out loud. He removed his fingers from my ass but left the dildo.

"You know," he said, firmly pushing himself up so he was looking down at me. Grabbing my nipple, he twisted. I whimpered but it wasn't from pain. I was starting to think he could make anything

- 59 -

pleasurable. "I'm starting to think you missed the part where I said torture until secrets started pouring out of your mouth like a waterfall." I started giggling at his awful pun. "If you're laughing I must need to get out the horse whip and electric cattle prod," he said looking even angrier. He must not find being laughed at during sex amusing.

"N-no," I stuttered, happy it was from laughing so hard and not from nerves for once. Managing to get my laughter mostly under control I said, "I-I'll talk. I swears to t-tells the truth, too!" I don't know why I was antagonizing him, except the more agitated he got the more I relaxed and the less I thought about my aching need for release. "Here's a secret, when I was ten I forgot to feed my pet rock, Rocky. He died and I felt so guilty I buried him out back and told my mom he ran away." He looked at me like he was trying to figure out what drug I was suddenly tripping on and how I got it while being tied to his bed. "Don't look at me like that, since that night I snuck out and buried Rocky, like he was nothing but a dead hooker, I have devoted my life to raising awareness for pet rocks. A pet rock is a serious commitment and too much responsibility for a ten year old to handle on his own," I somehow managed to say seriously.

"What the fuck? I don't care about no Goddamn pet rock, Moltenman. Tell me about the Gold Griffin Gemstone," he grinned mischievously, "or you'll wear that cock ring until your nuts fall off." I doubted he'd go that far but it wasn't a risk I was willing to take.

"Do you know nothing about the gem? Rocky was the Gold Griffin Gem. The spirit of the last Golden Griffin was contained in a rock. That rock had to be protected and the Griffin spirit needed nourishment to survive until the prophecy was fulfilled. The one who could control water was supposed to surround the rock with enough water and pressurized heat to break the hard shell. Then the spirit needed to be contained in a water cocoon, until it was strong enough to survive on its own. According to legend, it was supposed to be able to bring back The Golden Griffins but since I killed the spirit before I developed my powers." I shrugged like

I didn't wipe out an entire race of mythical beings. He just stared at me his mouth hanging open. He probably thinks I'm insane but, whatever, I answered his question, "Why did you want it?"

"It sounded pretty," he responded as he put his hand on my cheek, thankfully not the one that was in my ass a few minutes ago. "And I like pretty."

"I did you a favor then, this was the ugliest, dullest rock I have ever seen. You owe me for sparing you the sight of it." I liked talking to Brian like this. It was easy, I'll have to try it when I'm not tied up and naked.

"What do I owe you?" he asked slyly moving his hand back to my chest.

"You know"

"I think you should tell me, to make sure I reward you properly for telling me about Rocky and making sure I never had my retinas assaulted by the sight of him."

"I want to come but I want to do it with you inside me. I want you to fuck me until I can't walk."

"And you think that will be a suitable compensation?" he asked getting off the bed.

"It's a start," I said with my own grin. He started slowly taking off his costume, knowing I was mesmerized by his every move. With his top off, I think I started drooling, seeing his firm chest and muscular abs. He had a small trail of dark hair from his navel disappearing into his tights. I wanted to follow that trail with my tongue and get my mouth around that cock bulging in his tights.

"I'll be right back," he said stepping out of the little black room. He returned shortly saying, "Had to wash my hands," or something like that. I was distracted by the fact he returned naked, except for his mask. His cock was fully erect and sticking straight out. It was perfect and I wanted to taste it. He went over to his drawer and pulled out a condom.

"Wait," I stopped him before he started putting it on. "Let me taste you first." I surprised myself again by how firm my voice was and that I was even talking in almost complete sentences.

"Sorry but you're not the only one ready to blow," he didn't sound sorry as he finished rolling on the condom. Once he was between my legs he slowly removed the dildo from my ass. Tossing it aside, he coated his cock with lube. He lifted my legs and held them up so he had easy access to my hole. He positioned his knees on the sides of my ass. Looking at my ass, he slowly leaned forward. I felt his dick slide over my stretched entrance a couple of times.

Changing the angle of his rocking, I felt the head of his cock push inside my ass. I whimpered, his cock was stretching me more than his fingers and dildo had. Keeping a steady rhythm, he didn't stop until his balls were resting against my ass. He let go of my legs and I instinctively wrapped them around his waist, trying to pull him in even further. Leaning over me, he put his weight on his elbows and his lips against my ear, "I need a minute. The noises you were making earlier had me about coming in my pants. Now that I'm inside you, well, I won't be able to last very long." He sucked my earlobe into his mouth, gently nibbling at it before continuing, "You feel so good, I want to stay in you all night."

He leaned up and kissed me as he began to rock his hips gently, making shallow thrusts as his tongue invaded my mouth. His thrusts were slowly increasing in length and force. Soon he was pulling out of the kiss and leaning back onto his knees. He reached down and began to remove the cock ring. Finally. "I'm taking it off but you still can't come until I tell you to." I thought I'd try to hold off a little longer but there was no way I'd be able to wait much longer.

He tossed the cock ring to the floor and grabbed my legs under my thighs. He kept lifting them until I was bent in half with my cock hanging above my face, beyond that I could see Brian's incredible body and stare into his eyes. He had managed to get on his feet, was crouching so his dick never left my hole. Holding my legs, he began to thrust into me with long, hard strokes. We maintained eye contact as he pounded into me at a steady rate.

I had been on the edge of coming too long and didn't think I could hold back any longer. He must have seen the plea in my eyes. "Come," was all he said, all he needed to say. Before he even finished the word, I had my eyes closed and my cock was shooting its first burst of semen, landing across my chin and closed lips. It felt like I just kept coming, even after the spunk stopped pumping, my body still shuddered.

When my body finally relaxed, I opened my eyes and looked up at Brian, lost in his orgasm. His eyes were scrunched, his mouth open slightly, he looked quite pleased. Still wearing his Darkfist mask, he was the most erotic sight I'd ever seen. If I hadn't just blown what felt like two weeks of come on my own face, I'd probably have climaxed again just from watching him.

I opened my mouth and licked the come off my lips. I'd rather have it be Brian's come but in my current state of elation it didn't matter. My arms were still tied to the bed so I couldn't wipe the jizz off my face. It was starting to tickle as it dripped down my cheeks and neck.

"Brian," I said quietly, not wanting to interrupt his bliss but my face was starting to really bother me. He responded with an "Mmm?" so I continued, "I need my hands, my face is itchy."

He opened his eyes and smiled affectionately, he was stunning. "Sorry, babe, I'll take care of you." He grabbed the base of his dick and pulled out of me. I missed his cock filling me.

He removed the condom, tied it off and tossed it onto the floor. Gross. Brian wiped his hands on the blankets before leaning towards me. "You look hot with all that come on your face but next time I'll give you the facial." Then he leaned in and licked my come off my left cheek, then my chin and neck before cleaning the other cheek. Once he had my face clean, he put his mouth above mine, a few inches between us. Instead of swallowing my semen, he opened his lips and let the come dribble into my mouth.

I had to either swallow or let it run back out on my face. When he was done sharing, he swallowed before crushing my lips against his. He knew how to kiss and I could feel my cock getting hard again just from the way his tongue fucked my mouth. His hands worked on untying me while he continued to kiss me. When he pulled out of the kiss, he had untied my arms and was softly rubbing my wrists. He looked at them both and smiled. I pulled them down and noticed they weren't red or anything. My arm muscles were only a little stiff and my ass felt well fucked so I was very happy with how the party was going.

Lying down on his back beside me, he pulled me against him with my head on his chest. Luckily, he was on most of the dirty wet spots. He kissed the top of my head gently before asking, "Was it as good as your fantasy?"

"How did you know that was my fantasy? And it was far better than any fantasy I've ever had." I felt him smile against my head and pull me tighter against his chest.

"I read your Blog, I memorized your top ten fantasies and I plan on making sure they all come true. Even though you suck at role-playing, you make up for it being so cute and responsive. It's hard to believe you're so shy though when you post all those dirty fantasies on a public Blog."

I looked up at him, not sure what to say exactly, "I didn't think anyone read my Blog." He leaned down and gave me a quick kiss before pulling me back against his chest.

"I'm glad I read your Blog, now rest, I have a surprise for you when we wake up." I drifted off wondering which of my fantasies he'd planned for next, and if it was okay to nap wearing contacts? Shit.

Dirty Hero (A Dirty Zero Sequel)
Copyright© 2012 Kyle Adams

"Are they supposed to be unaware of our presence?" Darkfist whispered.

"You know they are," I grunted, annoyed he was acting so dumb tonight. He was up to something, although I couldn't figure out what. We were lying on our stomachs in the grass. The light from the almost full moon allowed me to see his stunning face and see how well his tights molded to his sculpted body. The curve of his ass made me uncomfortably hard in my own tights -my cock pressing against the ground was painful. We were on a mission to gather information on a mutual enemy and hoping we'd learn something useful to help formulate a plan. Even if we were on the same side momentarily, I still didn't trust Darkfist. This was the first time we'd seen each other since he kidnapped me and, well, tortured me. So what if I still jacked off remembering the things he did, it wouldn't happen again.

"I thought so. But, you're glowing like a fairy and they'll see you a mile away. Then our cover will be blown and I might have to punish your incompetence." I tried not to think about how hot it was being at his mercy and tried to remind myself that he was an asshole…and the enemy. It didn't work, my dick got stiffer and dug harder into the ground. I tried not to squirm or show any signs that he made me so achingly aroused.

By 'glowing', he meant my Moltenman costume. The flames blazed brightly in the darkness. "Well, since I'm pretending to be Moltenman, *He* would use his power to shield the glow. Pretend I'm doing that." I hated to break character since Brian liked to play scenes staying in character the whole time, but sometimes it couldn't be helped. I didn't know how to prevent the brightness radiating from my costume; I paid a shit load of money for this effect. Bad enough the costume was getting grass stains and now Darkfist was bitching about it.

"Since you're having issues controlling your concealment, you'll have to turn your costume inside out. You wouldn't want to fail because someone spotted your flaming aura, right?" The bastard knew failing wasn't an option, but reversing my costume didn't seem like a good alternative either.

"I think trying to maneuver out of the costume would draw more attention then just laying here." *Take that witty retort, Darkfist and shove it where my glowiness doesn't shine.*

"You look like a flare. A giant flaming beacon screaming 'Here We Are!' We won't be able to get close enough to learn anything. It's not *my* fault your pixie costume sucks at being stealthy." He sounded so irritated and that was impressive since he also remained so quiet.

"Whatever! Why don't you go spy on them? I'll watch your back from here, and come save you if something goes wrong." That sounded like a reasonable idea to me, even if it did seem a little childish coming from Moltenman.

"Fuck that! If I go in there alone there is no way I'm sharing any information I collect. So either change behind the trees so no one sees you flaunting around, or go home."

"You could have mentioned the suit glowed sooner, like *before* we got out here," I grunted as I started belly crawling over to the trees.

"How was I to know your powers would malfunction? And this way is more fun." I ignored him, just wanting to get it over with. The tree I crawled behind was old and had a wide trunk, so I was easily hidden. Standing up with my back towards the tree, I started trying to wiggle out of my costume. I was too uncoordinated and it was too tight to try and take it off quickly. If I did, then the sleeves would get jammed and I'd just end up trapped. I've tried hurrying to get it off before and it doesn't work.

- 66 -

A few minutes later I stood there naked, trying to quickly turn my tights inside out. I hoped the black lining would be dark enough for *His Majesty Darkfist*. Okay, I might've been bitching as I worked on changing, but I was pissed, mostly that he was right.

"Oh, just fucking peachy," I grunted noticing the small-ish white stain that had formed inside the crotch of my suit. Great, I'd have to finish the mission with come-stained pants. Of course, it'd be too much to hope Darkfist wouldn't notice. I should've worn a jock or something to absorb all the pre-come I leaked around Darkfist. But I hated how underwear made lines in my tights, so I always went commando. I wanted to at least clean it off so it wouldn't be as noticeable, but worried if I tried to wipe it off I'd just smear it around and make it worse. Maybe I could lick it clean. Then it would just be wet and not as noticeable on the black fabric.

All my thinking stopped when I was slammed against the tree. I grunted when my bare skin hit the rough bark. I didn't have time to react before Darkfist had my wrists pinned against the tree over my head. His hard body pressed against mine as he whispered in my ear, "Looks like I got you excited and you made a mess in your pants."

"Don't flatter yourself. I'm always excited and making a mess." Wow, that sounded a lot better in my head. *Still* better to sound like an insatiable and somewhat sloppy sex fiend than to have him think he was the reason for my premature leakage.

"You know, we have at least 30 minutes before anything happens, let's make good use of the time," he all but purred in my ear.

"No, we don't, something could happen any minute now and we have to get ourselves into position. Superheroes don't have sex during missions." I was proud of how confident my voice sounded. Maybe I could pull off the Moltenman persona and stay in character after all.

"You should know by now I'm not a superhero, I'm the charming and irresistible villain. Bad guys take what they want, and right now all I want is you," he said, sucking my earlobe between his lips. He nibbled on it a little before trailing kisses down my neck. I couldn't help moaning, his lips were magical. If he didn't have my hands held firmly above my head, I would've grabbed his hair and pulled his lips tighter to my skin. I could have climaxed just from having him suck on my neck it felt so good. The slight discomfort of the bark against my back was long forgotten. I knew by this point I wasn't doing a very good job of being Moltenman, but Darkfist made me lose all self-control.

I couldn't help but whine when he stopped and pulled his head back. "You better be quiet or you'll alert the enemy of our presence." I opened my mouth to, you know, yell at him for making me *make* noise but he crushed his lips against mine before I could.

His kiss was animalistic. He shoved his tongue in my mouth, tangling it with my own. He pressed his hard cock to mine and started thrusting them against each other firmly. All the while he kept kissing his way along my jaw until he got to my ear and whispered, "When I let go of your hands put them behind your head and leave them there until I say you can move them."

I put my hands behind my head the second I felt his hold release. I caught a brief smile on his face and watched as he dropped to his knees in front of me. Wasting no time, he inhaled my cock, not stopping until his nose was buried in my trimmed pubic hair. The surprise of the sensation made my knees buckle - even leaning against the tree, I would have fallen if not for his gloved hands holding my hips steady. The wicked things he could do with his mouth left me gasping for air. It didn't help that as he worked my cock with his tongue and lips he slowly caressed my stomach with his hands. He was slowly sliding them towards my chest, I had no idea the leather gloves would feel so different. My skin tingled in the trail they left. I jumped again when they got to my nipples, gently rubbing and twisting. It was too much, I was too ready; I wasn't going to last thirty seconds with his mouth on me and those gloves driving spikes of pleasure throughout my whole body with every pinch and twist.

"Oh, fuck. Don't stop, so close, oh fuck," I kept murmuring. I was close, a few more minutes and I'd erupt in his mouth. Sensing my quickly approaching climax, he pulled his mouth off my cock and his hands stopped playing with my nipples. I grunted in frustration, even though I should've known he wouldn't let me come so soon.

"You can't come until I'm inside you, but I won't make you wait long." He was close enough that I could see the mischievous glint in his eyes as the moonlight reflected off them. He was the most handsome man I'd ever seen, and the dark mask around his eyes was beyond erotic. He could get me to do anything and he knew it too, judging by the way he was smirking at me. "Turn around, put your hands flat on the tree and bend forward." I didn't even think about it, just got into the position as he ordered.

I felt him step up behind me and place his hands on my shoulders. He kneaded them a couple times before slowly dragging them down my back. My body shivered when I felt him start to massage my ass, I thought I was quickly developing some kind of leather fetish. I'd think more about that later when a leather covered finger wasn't working its way down my ass crack. I heard him inhale sharply and felt his finger press against the plug in my ass. I think he liked my surprise. I couldn't help but gasp when he pressed harder against the base, working the plug deeper inside me.

"Someone was planning ahead, naughty Moltenman." he said huskily as he grabbed the plug by the base and pulled it almost all the way out before shoving it back in. He did this a few times, rotating it as he pushed and pulled it from my body. It felt incredible but I was aching for it to be his cock pumping into me instead. "That's so hot, I could look at that plug fucking your ass forever, but *I* need to fuck you now," he whispered as he pulled the plug out and tossed it on the ground. He shifted behind me and I felt his cock slide up my crease, when he reached my opening, he slowly pushed in. After waiting a few seconds with just his head in, he thrust forward until his hips were pressed snug against my ass.

I could feel his tights pressing against the back of my thighs; he didn't remove them just pulled them down enough to free his cock. He had to bend his legs to make up for our height difference. I felt him lean over my body, the diamonds from the front on his costume slightly pressed against my back. It didn't hurt, it felt fucking amazing; he wasn't putting any weight on my back, and the light pressure made my skin tingle, like several tiny points stimulating my sensitive skin. He put one hand on my shoulder and the other on my hip, he was planning to make this a rough ride. *Fuck,* I liked it rough. "I'm going to fuck you so hard you'll want to scream, but if you so much as moan I might not let you come." He growled into my ear as he squeezed my shoulder. "Better hold on because I'm going to pound you through this fucking tree."

I had to bite my lip to keep myself from moaning. His thrusts were gentle at first, he was just getting into his rhythm and quickly the speed and force of his thrusts picked up. He was driving his cock into me hard enough to make my feet bounce off the ground. It took all of my upper arm strength to keep from being rammed into the tree. "Fuck, I love fucking your tight ass," he grunted in my ear as he continued to forcefully ram his thick cock into me.

It wasn't long before I felt his hand drift from my hip to my cock. "You've been so quiet I think I should let you come." He wrapped his gloved fist around my throbbing cock. "I want to feel your ass tighten around my cock before I fill it with my own come." He started pumping my cock in rhythm with his deep thrusting, within three strokes I was coming, hard. I'm not sure how long after my orgasm started before Darkfist had his own release. When my senses returned, he was resting fully inside of me and brushing kisses along my shoulder and neck.

He brought his hand up to my face. "You made a mess on my glove, clean it." I stuck my tongue out and started licking his glove clean.

Honestly, the leather didn't taste good but cleaning his glove soaked in my come was too hot for me to care. I licked it thoroughly, being careful around the diamond studs along the back. I didn't want to cut my tongue.

When I had all the come off his glove, he brought his hand down to my stomach and started rubbing in small circles. We stayed like that for a few minutes before he spoke, "I think we took too long, with my super hearing I heard them drive off about ten minutes ago."

"You don't have super hearing," I replied sarcastically.

"With my slightly better than average hearing then," he retorted.

"So we failed?" I left off the 'because of you' since I hadn't really put up much resistance.

"I feel pretty successful actually," he shrugged coolly.

"What was the mission again? I feel like I should be worried we failed but can't bring myself to care. I think you're rubbing off on me."

"I'll rub off on you later; need a little time to recover first. You're right. You are the worst superhero, like ever. Letting millions die while letting the enemy fuck your tight ass. Shame on you, Moltenman."

"I think social etiquette dictates to at least pull your cock out of someone's ass before you insult them. Don't be rude, Darkfist."

He laughed and slowly pulled out. "Lay in the grass with me?" he asked. We were done playing if he wasn't ordering me around. I had done pretty well, only broke character once. I turned around and walked the few feet over to where he was laying down on his back. I wished he was naked so I could lie on top of him, but he still wore his costume, his pants still pulled down to his upper thighs. He was gorgeous.

Lying down on my side next to him I rested my head on his chest. Brian wrapped his arm around me and pulled me tighter against him. "That's what, four now?" Brian asked.

"More like three and a half," I replied, being a little snarky.

"Why only three point five? There was the first time when we got together and I tied you up. And then there's the fantasy where you are at work jerking off in the bathroom and I catch you and help you finish. How many times have I made that one come true? Sometimes twice in one day even."

"Thirty-four times, but you always get me so worked up that I have to go to the bathroom to get relief. I can't work all day with an erection! And you can only cross it off the list once, doing it anymore after that is just for fun." And fun we've had. I can't go into the bathroom at work without popping a boner.

"Then there was getting fucked in the rain on the deck of a boat. I had to get a boat license for that one, which should be extra credit or something," Brian said sounding a little smug, deservedly so.

"No extra credit since you enjoyed it as much as I did," I replied, remembering the weekend on the houseboat Brian rented. I can't even think about boats without my cock getting stiff.

"And then tonight makes four."

"Except in my fantasy we didn't fail the mission and we played a lot more. We had just gotten down on the grass and the first thing you said to me was about how my outfit was flaming and to turn it inside out. In my fantasy, we got the information we needed and then fucked in a ventilation shaft or in some hiding place."

"Wait, let me make sure I understand this. Because we only made it to the backyard and I didn't wait long enough for you to imagine people were meeting about some villainess scheme, tonight only counts as half a fantasy completed?"

"Yeah, it's half a point, or if you want a letter grade it's an E for Effort. You wouldn't want me to change my fantasy just so your attempt to perform it was successful would you?"

"No, of course not, I'll make sure next time you have plenty of time to crawl around before anything sexual happens so the integrity of the fantasy is upheld."

"I knew you'd understand," I said sounding a little sleepy, no way I'd let myself fall asleep though. I didn't sleep with contacts in my eyes, it can lead to an infection and it's not pretty. I'll never make that mistake again, for the whole first week Brian and I were together, my left eye was a disgusting, bloodshot mess. I thought for sure he'd dump me before it healed, but he stuck by me and my nasty eye. Surprisingly, my right eye was fine and only my left eye had a vendetta to try and ruin my life by attempting to scare Brian away. Luckily it wasn't too severe and some expensive as gold-shit eye drops cleared it up. Tonight was the first time I'd worn contacts since the night Brian and I got together, and no matter how tired I was, there was no way I'd fall asleep with demon-lenses in my eyes again. Not even wrapped in Brian's tender embrace could I be lured into sleep while wearing contacts.

Brian increased the pressure on his arm, pulling me even tighter against him. We continued to just lay there for a few minutes. "Six months. Best six months of my life," he said quietly before he pressed his lips against my forehead.

"Mine too," I whispered back. Hard to believe how much could change in six months. I rarely stuttered anymore, only when Brian really surprised me and I got flustered. Like last week when he suggested we get tested to do away with the condoms. "For economical reasons," he said, with as much sex as we were having, the condom budget was getting astronomical. Or like last night when he suggested we move in together, I eventually stammered my way through the surprise and agreed. Luckily, he thought my stutter was cute.

The best part of the night was after dinner when he brought me home and we made love for hours. It was slow and intimate, gentle caresses and staring into each other's eyes. Our first time without a condom, when we were both finished, he leaned down and whispered for the first time, "I love you, Wyatt."

It was nice hearing the words but I already knew he loved me by the little things he did. Like, how he was always grabbing my hand or how he looked at me and smiled as if I was the most important thing in the world. Every Friday, even though we went to lunch together, there was always a single long stemmed rose on my keyboard when I got back to my desk. With a little note attached promising the best weekend of my life. So far, he had yet to disappoint. Every day with Brian got better.

I wasn't quite as romantically creative as Brian, but I hoped when he saw me looking at him and smiling like a dork, he knew he was the most important person in my world, too. I did make him write me a list of his top ten fantasies. I thought the only fair thing to do was to make his desires come true the way he had mine. And the man was like a sex god, so there was no hardship worshiping him every chance I got. Of course, he had to show me up and have fifteen fantasies. That was okay because I had some new fantasies to add to my list, maybe something with leather chaps and a motorcycle.

THE END

An Introduction to Love Is Always Write

The story you are about to read celebrates love, sex and romance between men. It is a product of the Love Is Always Write Event sponsored by the Goodreads M/M Romance group and is published as a free gift to you.

What Is Love Is Always Write?

The Goodreads M/M Romance group invited members to choose a photo and pen a letter asking for a short M/M romance story inspired by the image; authors from the group were encouraged to select a letter and write an original tale. The result was an outpouring of creativity that shined a spotlight on the special bond between M/M romance writers and the people who love what they do.

A written description of the image that inspired this story is provided along with the original request letter. If you'd like to view the photo, please feel free to join the Goodreads M/M Romance group and visit the discussion section: Love Is Always Write. Link to Story Prompt at Goodreads

STORY PROMPT:

It's easy to be a hero in the game. When we play together, I'm brave and strong and handsome and I slay the dragon. But when we stop playing, I'm back to being regular old me.

Am I brave enough to tell him how I feel? When the game ends, can we still be comrades in arms, or is it all just empty fantasy?

SUBMITTED BY: Joanna

Dirty Play

Copyright© 2012 Kyle Adams

Author Note: Role-Playing Games (RPGs) are about storytelling so during the game scenes I left out the dice rolling and experience/hit point tracking, etc. to keep it more of a smooth story.

****

The first time he showed up was for our Tuesday night game. We played every Tuesday and Thursday at *Games You Play*. Not the most creative name but it was the largest game store in Syracuse. They had the best selection of books, character pieces, and pretty much every game and expansion pack available. If they didn't have something, they could order it. The store had an open floor plan: the products were in the front and eight gaming tables were set up in the back.

I was sitting in my usual spot at one of the tables, facing the front of the store so I could watch people as they came and went. I should add emphasis to the word 'could' because I never paid attention to anything but the game. That's why I was surprised when I heard a deep voice call out, "Hey, Jayne, sorry I'm a little late." I stopped setting my game stuff up and looked up to see who was talking to Jayne. The guy was gorgeous. He was probably about six-feet, and I could tell his body was solid under his form-fitting leather jacket. His shaved head revealed his smooth, chocolaty skin. I just gawked at him, wondering if he would taste as good as he looked.

"You're fine, sweetie. We haven't even gotten set up yet." Jayne smiled at him, "Everyone this is Zack. He'll be joining us. Zack, that's Brett, he's our thief," Jayne said while pointing to Brett, who was sitting beside me. Moving on to me, "The pale, scrawny guy is Whitney, and he is our warrior."

Hearing my full first name helped me stop staring and shift my gaze to glare at Jayne. "Please call me Whit. Whitney is my mother." Jayne completely ignored me as she moved onto the next introduction.

"And that is Randy. He plays a mage. You can sit next to him." She gestured towards the empty chair across from me.

Jayne was the Game Master so she always took charge, sitting at the end of the table where she had enough room for all of her stuff. She had her Master's screen up blocking everyone at the table from seeing what books or charts she had out. She got very into the game and liked all the traps, quests, or attacks to be completely unexpected. She was the best Game Master I'd ever played with. She always planned ahead and kept all the players on their toes. Judging by how confused Brett and Randy looked, I guessed I wasn't the only one wondering why Zack was here.

Randy and Brett both said, "Nice to meet you," but I was feeling more shy than usual and pretended to study my character sheet while I quietly mumbled, "Hi." Besides, I already told him to call me Whit, even if I *was* looking at Jayne while I said it.

I couldn't concentrate on my character. I'd already planned out my next three level-ups but it didn't hurt to go over them again and make sure they were the most strategically beneficial. All I could think about was how the hunk across from me made my cock hard.

"It's nice to meet you guys as well. Thanks for letting me join while you're in the middle of a game." Zack's deep voice was sexier than anything I could imagine. I felt like he had whispered dirty things in my ear. I was so distracted by the way his voice made my skin tingle that it took me a second to process what he actually said. He was going to join the game and be here every week? How was I *ever* going to concentrate on the game?

"We should be thanking you for joining, Zack. This is going to make the game so much more fun," Jayne said excitedly. I had no idea what she was talking about; the game was already awesome with just the four of us. "Now that there are four players you can split up and go on multiple missions simultaneously. This will really help me strengthen my Game Master skills. I'm practicing for next year's national RPGM championship, as you all know."

"What's a RPGM?" Zack asked. I fought the urge to introduce my palm to my face at the realization the tall, dark hottie was a total newb.

"Role Play Game Master." Brett spoke slowly and over-enunciated every word.

"I'm not stupid, man, just new and don't know acronyms yet," Zack responded a little defensive, understandably since Brett spoke to him like he was a baby.

"You're new? You don't say." Randy sounded a little bitter, probably because we would be spending more time trying to teach Zack how to play for the next couple of weeks than we would actually playing the game. I figured with them talking I could safely steal a look at Zack without anyone noticing.

Mission: Sneak a Peek at Zack was a Fail. When I looked up he was staring right at me. When our eyes met he just lifted his eyebrow. *Fuck*, he was hot. I was pretty sure that eyebrow lift was challenging me to also comment on his nonexistent RPG knowledge. I said nothing and instead just smiled slightly and lowered my head, hoping no one would notice I was starting to blush. I wasn't sure where the idea came from, but as soon as I saw his eyebrow arch, all I could think about was running my tongue along that smooth curve. I was in trouble if I thought his brow was sexy.

Luckily, no one was paying attention to me as Jayne took over again. "Stop being babies! Yes, this is Zack's first time, but we were all new our first time, too. Don't worry, Zack, I'll make sure you understand everything and that none of these brats take advantage of your lack of experience. To start, you need to create a character, but before that we've got to go over the basic rules and game structure. Hopefully you'll know what kind of character you want to create afterward. We can loan you dice, a character piece, and stuff."

I sat there and listened patiently as Jayne started going over all the basics. Then she started going over everything on the character sheet. Character sheets are long and Jayne would be very detailed in explaining it. Knowing it would take a while, I pulled a drawing pad out of my bag and started doodling. Unfortunately, my thoughts about Zack were pretty heavy and my doodles were turning out X-rated. I closed my pad and put it away before someone noticed what I was sketching. I should try to pay attention anyway. Even if I wasn't ready to talk in front of Zack, I could at least try to look like I was providing moral support. I knew there was a reason to listen even if I wasn't sure what it was.

"Um, so are the little figures walking in a forest or something?" Zack asked, looking at the large game board on the table. It was marked with one inch squares and our three character pieces were standing on it. We could write on the board with dry erase markers and add other game objects. But the game was mostly all imagination so we tended to have a pretty blank board, mostly using it to mark character/item placements and track movements.

"More like a deserted waste land." Randy rolled his eyes like it should have been obvious where we were.

"Shouldn't there be traps or treasure chests or something?" Zack asked, examining the board closer.

"There wouldn't be a trap marked until after we discovered it, and we tend to raid chests when we find them, not mark it and have to go back later." Brett sounded bored and a little condescending. "Just because we can write on the board doesn't mean we have to."

"Oh, well, do things at least jump out at you?" I could listen to Zack ask questions all night, but looking around the table, I was pretty sure I was the only one. Brett looked so bored I thought he might leave. Jayne seemed like she was trying not to get frustrated, scrunching her face and trying to force it to relax, but she just looked constipated. She liked to teach without being interrupted and didn't like questions until the end. Randy just sat there coming across like, well, himself.

"Sometimes dark and sinister creatures lurk in the shadows, waiting to strike." Randy tried to sound eerie using his deepest voice. I watched as he grabbed his drink and started shaking it in front of the small figures in the middle of the game board. "Rawr! I'm a giant can of diet soda. Prepare to die, motherfuckers!" Then he made machine gun blasts as he used the base of the can to knock over the character pieces.

I snorted loudly. I folded my arms on the table and rested my head on them, trying to stop laughing. *Mission: Don't Embarrass Myself.* Fail. *Mission: Remain Mysteriously Quiet Through the Night.* Fail. Dog fucking damn it. Why did I have to snort? Randy isn't even that funny, and instead of a cool chuckle, I snorted like a damn farm animal. *Mission Update: Make it Through Rest of Night without Further Humiliating Myself.*

Luckily, they went back into helping Zack build his character after settling down from Randy's soda act. I'll admit I was a little jealous of Randy's ability to speak around strangers and make friends and be funny. I could be funny, probably, if I wasn't too scared to talk around people, especially people I found extremely attractive. I kept my head down, listening as Jayne explained our characters to Zack. Hopefully he would choose to be something different and complementary to our characters.

I played Cable, a strong, well-spoken human warrior who was skilled with blades but preferred longswords. He wore heavy armor most of the time but underneath I envisioned a strong body with bulging muscles. Cable was confident and didn't hesitate when making a decision. Basically, Cable was everything I wasn't.

Randy was a mage and wore traditional robes and amulets. He called his character Randy; yeah, Randy was just Randy. He was pretty original like that. He said it was because his character acts like he would if he could hurl fire-bolts or raise the dead.

Brett's character was a rogue, but in real life he worked at a bank. I don't know how to picture his character. He was always changing to blend in with his surroundings. His character is Rc, but he won't tell anyone what Rc means. It just adds to his character's complexity, he said.

We were all male characters, which was why Jayne tried to pressure Zack into making his character female, going on about how useful a female character would be, using her womanly wiles to help get discounts from shopkeepers or flirt with unsuspecting travelers (while the rest of us looted their shit). Of course, she was more persuasive than that.

"That's cool, I'll play a female," Zack readily agreed. I was surprised by how willing he was to play a female. Not that there was anything wrong with playing a female; he just looked so strong and manly. Yet he had no problem helping out the team and seemed rather excited about the whole thing.

"What race and class do you want to be?" Jayne questioned.

"I will be a cleric dark gnome named Sapphire," Zack said smugly. I was impressed he knew exactly what he wanted to be, even if gnomes were creepy little devils.

Randy sighed heavily, "It's race then class, newb. 'Dark gnome cleric' is how you should say it."

"Who cares how he said he wants to be a gnome? I'm more concerned with how that's supposed to be a 'devious distraction'," Brett reasoned, using air quotes, "when people won't even see you unless you stand on a stool?" Brett obviously didn't like the idea of having a female gnome on the team.

"Maybe I'll wear steel armor platform boots with spiked toes. And maybe you'll notice when I kick you in the nuts." Zack paused, taking a deep breath. "Sorry, I really got into character. Sapphire may be small, but she's spunky and won't put up with shit from anyone."

"Okay, this should be an interesting new addition to the game. Zack, please don't kick me in the vagina for asking, but I'm curious why you chose to be a gnome?" Jayne inquired.

"Why wouldn't I pick a gnome? They are so adorable and tiny. Oh, and they have the cutest hats." Was Zack on crack? Gnomes weren't cute... they were terrifying. My grandma had gnomes in her flower garden and all they did was scare kids off the lawn. And the clothes were just tragic, no style or coordination. And the hats? Those were just long and pointy and split your face open if you ever fell on one.

At least I knew Zack was most likely gay now. I was convinced he was at least sixty-eight percent gay. What kind of straight man would talk about gnome couture? Still, his level of taste left a lot to be desired, gay or straight. Maybe it was just wishful hoping that he would be gay and single and have a thing for socially-awkward nerds. Sure, his gnome-loving was creepy, but he was hot so it evened out. I could definitely tolerate small doses of gnome-speak if it meant getting to watch the way Zack smiled and used his hands to describe them.

"I even have a gnome keychain," I heard Zack say before I tuned out the creepy gnome talk. I had endured all the gnome-ness I could handle for now. I hated gnomes, and I'd probably have wet nightmares about them as it was. I could see the dream in my head: Zack has me pinned against the wall, my arms wrapped around his neck and my legs locked around his waist. We're naked, of course, and he is pounding his cock into me, and just when we're about to come, poorly dressed gnome terrorists show up with spoons. Gnomes liked spoons for scooping eyeballs out of skulls; they were that evil. I'd wake up once they started to hack my eyeless head off. I'd lay awake with my cock achingly hard while crying from the terror of the gnome attack. I would probably end up needing to double my therapy sessions. Maybe I just wouldn't sleep tonight, that would be safest. *New Mission: Find Something to do to Avoid Sleeping.*

It was going to be tough playing with a gnome, especially a female one that speaks in Zack's husky-man voice. He didn't even try to make it higher when he was in character (and usually threatening bodily harm). It was weird imagining a two-foot female fashion-disaster victim talking in such a manly voice. If gnomes weren't so scary I'd have laughed about it. I needed to find something to say to Zack and hope once I started the conversation, I could keep it going.

I started making lists in my head of stuff that was okay to say and what wasn't. Like "how's it going?" was good. "Want a blowjob?" was slightly too slutty and went on my 'don't say' list. "What do you think of the game so far?" was good, and in theory I should be able to talk about the game for hours. So I kept trying to find stuff to say, and then I had to work on actually saying it.

****

Mission: Talk to Zack had been going nowhere for three months now. Not only could I not talk to him, but Zack was distracting. He always wore tight t-shirts that stretched across his muscular chest. The game store was always a little chilly and shortly after he would slip out of his leather jacket, his nipples would both firm into points. Three months of imagining what it would be like rubbing—or preferably licking—that amazing chest and playing with those perky nipples.

Whenever I was caught staring, I would just look back at the board and feel myself blush. Sometimes when I accidentally made contact with his sultry brown eyes, he would give me a quirky half smile. I could tell by his smirk he knew I wanted him, but I just couldn't get the courage to actually say anything. It was so easy to watch him, wishing I could find the courage to ask him to get coffee or something. Then I'd think, "what if he said yes?" I'd spend the whole time stumbling through, trying to figure out more things to say—and subtly imply I was *up* for more than just coffee—without being too direct in case he wasn't gay. It didn't take much for me to talk myself out of asking him to hangout.

I was convinced that there was at least a seventy-three percent chance he was gay. I bumped it up from sixty-eight after our third game. Zack showed up wearing a light pink shirt that was tighter than usual. 'It's All Geek To Me' was written across the chest, the serif font appearing elongated from how much the fabric had to stretch. Then the next game he was wearing a black shirt that said "Go ahead, play with my" followed by a picture of an old Atari joystick. Zack had caught me staring at his chest enough that he had to know I'd see it, but I wasn't sure if the shirt was a serious invitation, if he was just teasing me, or if he even wore it for me.

If he was trying to tease me, it worked. His shirts did nothing but inspire my imagination and make me want him even more. It wasn't just that he was physically the epitome of my every desire, but I genuinely liked him, what I knew of him.

I really hadn't talked to him beyond mumbled "hellos," but I did manage to talk to him in the game. That was Cable talking to Psychotic Gnome AKA Sapphire, which was just me, teasing. I got over my fear of gnomes, in the game at least, but I still can't go to my grandma's house without having a minor panic attack. Even though Sapphire didn't terrify me any longer, I still enjoyed making fun of her or having Cable do it for me.

Playing with Zack was fun. Besides being able to tease Sapphire, he really did make things more interesting. He always had something snarky to say to any baddies we encountered. He was also a very supportive team player. As snarky as he was to the villains, he always had something supportive to say to the team even though we all still teased him about making newb moves. He was always using his turn to heal one of us, even if he had more exciting things he could be doing. As sweet as I thought it was that he always looked out for the team, I enjoyed it more when he went off on the creatures. The stuff he would shout at them never failed to make me laugh. Who can resist a hot guy that looks out for his own and makes you laugh?

Unfortunately, even as Cable, my in-game conversations never went the way I wanted them to. Like last week, Cable told Sapphire she could use a bath—because she smelled like shit and was covered in slime from the fourteen-headed snot-slug she stupidly sliced open. (Everyone knew you killed those with a ranged attack.) Anyway, what I wanted Cable to say was, "Even covered in avocado snot and chunks of withering slug flesh, you still take my breath away. Not from the putrid odor either, but because your beauty shines through even the thickest secretions." And then Cable would kiss those slime-covered gnome lips… or some deeply romantic gesture like that.

This time would be different though, Sapphire got herself in trouble, and when Cable strutted in there to save her, he was going to say something smooth and flirty. *Newest Mission: Flirt with Zack by Using Cable.*

Maybe now would be a good time to point out I don't have split personalities. My new therapist, Nerey, told me that. I knew I controlled Cable, and Nerey said something about how I was just insecure and projecting all my confidence and esteem into the character of Cable, and I should work on focusing that confidence internally. I thought she was full of shit, but I liked talking to her. Something about paying her for her time made me open up. And I liked how instead of calling me a shy chicken, she would say I have a "nervous anxiety disorder preventing me from initiating communication with Zack," or something fancy like that. I thought she was enabling me to remain distant more than actually helping me get past the anxiety. Maybe I needed a new therapist. Maybe I should've looked into getting a team of them?

I thought about offering to pay Zack to see if that would help me relax enough to talk. *Mission: Pay Zack* was quickly marked 'Too Risky' and terminated. Knowing me, I'd probably think I was being sly and say something like, "How's fifty bucks for an hour sound?" and he would think I was insinuating he was a whore and punch me in the face. That was the best case scenario, so no offering Zack compensation for his time.

None of that matters now, though, because the game was going to let me be a hero. Randy and Rc were off searching for a juju or something in some underwater caverns. Cable's not part of that storyline, so trust me, it was boring. While they were off swimming, Sapphire and Cable were trudging through the forsaken desert lands. We were searching for the Rod of Improbability. It was believed to be in the upside-down pyramid in the liver of the desert's death oasis. The desert wasn't an easy place to pass through and got tougher the closer you got to the liver. If gnomes could swim, Sapphire would be on the other mission since it was far easier. Easier as in boring. Luckily she couldn't swim and was privileged enough to get rescued by Cable, repeatedly. That is, until this morning, day four in this hellacious desert.

The worst thing imaginable happened. Okay, that was a little dramatic. Sapphire was kidnapped from her sleeping shelter. She was probably being beaten and tortured. I wouldn't be surprised if she was being strung up by her ankles and having her skin melted off, slowly. I knew it was just awful, but I smiled thinking this was the best thing ever. Now Cable would get to really save his gnome and be the knight in abused armor.

That morning, just before the sun was to rise, Cable was awoken from his sleep by the low-pitched mannish screams of Sapphire. Cable thought to himself, *she probably saw a spider and is freaking out*, but spiders would seem a lot larger to one so small. Still lying in his bedding,

Cable began assessing the situation. Sapphire continued shrieking loud enough it could wake the dead.

It was impossible to sleep in heavy armor, so he was only wearing a pair of snug grey pants when he pulled himself out of bed. They were snug enough to show off the muscles in his legs but flexible enough to allow unrestricted movement. He grabbed his trusty longsword, Rel-Lik. (That's 'killer' spelled backwards.) Rel-Lik is long, narrow, and extremely sharp. It was just an ugly old sword. Rel-Lik had no magic enhancements or skill modifiers. It didn't need them. Very few creatures survived without their head; it didn't need to be anything more than sharp.

Cable left his armor in the tent. If it was just a spider, he planned to sleep a little longer after Princess-Gnome shut up. If something was seriously wrong, there wasn't time to mess with the armor. The screaming finally stopped. Sapphire probably fainted from fright. (I didn't see how anything could be more terrifying than a gnome, but I guessed everything had phobias.)

On alert, Cable silently exited his small tent, quickly noticing something was indeed wrong. The camp was being attacked and it looked like Sapphire was the target. Now that Cable was outside, he could hear Sapphire had stopped screaming and was hurling insults at her attackers. She may not have been able to put up much of a fight physically but at least she could give even the most secure creature a complex. It was hard to stay in character and not laugh as Sapphire told one of the Draczards— an androgynous man-snake-lizard-like thing—"Is that all you got, you beady-eyed son of a bitch? My gnome-nana hits harder than you, and she is over 400 years old, pussyface!"

"Someone gag the gnome, please. Her manly shrieking is making my ears bleed," one of the ugly green lizard creatures hissed. It was then Cable noticed this wasn't an attack per se, but they were trying to kidnap little Sapphire. They were trying to stuff her in an old bristly potato sack, but she was too slippery and it looked like she was biting them if they got near her mouth.

Why kidnap her? They couldn't possibly plan to ransom her back to us and expect us to pay, could they? Just listen to the shrill man-voice of the shrieking harpy. Why would anyone pay to get that back? Who was Cable trying to kid? Sapphire was part of the team and he'd do whatever it took to get her back. Still, they couldn't have known that; they must want her for something else—need her alive—or they would have already killed her... probably need her blood or skin for some ancient curse or other dark ritual. Cable almost felt bad for the kidnappers; no one deserved the verbal abuse Sapphire could spit out.

Cable resisted the urge to let out a battle cry and rush to save Princess-Gnome-Stool. Cable was too smart to give away his advantage: no one had noticed he was there, yet. There were eight of the creepy walking lizards, and without his armor or reinforcements, he'd need the surprise and hopefully take out two of them before they even realized he was there. Normally Cable wouldn't have liked killing someone from behind, but it was eight against one and his sleep had been interrupted so he was cranky.

In situations like this, things rarely go as planned. When it comes down to it, it is all luck of the dice. Cable's first swing with Rel-Lik was aimed to decapitate the monster closest to him. Swinging with a strong, quick strike, he... missed. There went the advantage of a surprise attack. *Bitch fucker whore!* Cable didn't say that out loud. He was a silent fighter; to show frustration would just make him look weak, and taunting sounded desperate. Cable liked to remain unyielding and let nothing show on his face. Without armor, Cable couldn't afford to take any chances. Even if his movement would be a lot quicker without the heavy burden of armor, he'd have to fight defensively, which could take awhile.

Avoiding their long, spiky teeth and the eight razor claws they had on each limb was vital to coming out victorious. Three of the

Draczards closest to Cable broke away from the pack and each took a turn trying to score a hit. They missed. Cable responded quickly and thrust Rel-Lik into the nearest lizard's upper body, piercing the thick-scaled chest plate. Wrenching the sword into the vulnerable organs, Cable watched as the lizard's thick, yellow-orangey blood began to bubble between the creature's nasty teeth. Ripping his sword out, Cable watched the thing fall lifelessly to the sand. He didn't know much about the Draczards' biology, but he approached every fight the same: stab it, and if it didn't die, cut its head off. It had worked well so far.

The remaining two attacked at once. Cable dodged the first one but the second connected with the back of his left shoulder, leaving eight shallow claw marks. At least the hit had only grazed him, and Cable was right-handed, so he could still use Rel-Lik unhindered. He needed to wrap this up, and fast. Dodging two more attacks, Cable was able to retaliate and drive his sword through the lizard's left eye. Rel-Lik slid out smooth and clean.

Draczards had thick mucus-like blood that would stretch and snap back, leaving the blade mostly blood-free. Even the strongest stomach could become weak when assaulted with being covered in slime and guts, nostrils filled with putrid, nauseating odors. As long as one avoided the teeth and claws, Draczards were an easy, no-mess kill, a huge help when there was a large group of them to slaughter for messing with your gnome. She might have been loud, mostly useless, and always getting in trouble, but she was Cable's useless gnome, dammit, and no one messed with something of Cable's.

Before the Draczard's body had hit the sand Cable had spun around, and in one swift motion Rel-Lik sliced through the remaining lizard's neck. Cable watched as the body crumpled and the head rolled a few times, coming to a stop in an upright position a few feet away.

Well, bloody fucking shit snatchers, Cable thought to himself. They were gone; the remaining five Draczards had escaped with their hapless victim, Sapphire. Well just fucking great, now a rescue mission would need to be devised. At least he would still be able to be the hero, rescue Sapphire, and get the perfect opportunity to flirt and be charming.

The desert sun had risen and there were a few fluffy clouds in the azure sky. It was a bright morning, but Cable was infuriated. With the rusty desert rock cliffs to his back and no one around to bear witness, Cable allowed himself to expel his frustrations. He drove Rel-Lik into the sand next to the pile of Draczard remains. His body tensed and his muscles bulged as he clenched his teeth. Channeling all of his irritation through his taut body, he let it out in a long, animalistic roar.

"Jesus, Whitney, stop fucking screaming already." I barely heard Randy trying to yell over me. And fuck him, I wasn't screaming, I was roaring like a savage beast that just had its gnome kidnapped. Huge difference between that and screaming! I did stop *roaring* though, as he was right, I was a little loud. But I was just in character.

"Okay, that's a good place to finish for the night," Jayne said as she started gathering her stuff. What the hell, we couldn't stop there! Cable was going to save Sapphire and be smooth with the whole flirting thing. Yeah, he was going to have her eating out of his hand, and by association Zack would want me just as much as Sapphire would want Cable. Fuck, no way could I wait for Tuesday to continue. I'd drive myself insane and lose all my nerve by then.

There was no point arguing and asking to continue as they were all chattering and getting their stuff put away. I was always the first one to leave after the game ended. I liked playing with the gang but I didn't really talk to them much in the outside world. Emails were exchanged and new ideas brought up, sometimes strategies were discussed, but for the most part we just played the game. Zack was the only one I wanted to get to know *better*, but how could I when just being near him makes me drool, and actually talking to him, I'd probably shit my pants.

I quickly gathered my few books and game equipment. I turned to stuff them in my bag but it was gone. I always left my bag leaning against the metal leg of my chair. So where the hell was it? I checked the right side, just in case. Not there either, not that I really expected it to be. I never noticed anyone come over to our table, but I really get into the game. I doubted someone had walked over and jacked my bag while we all just sat here. I did a quick scan of the room trying to see if I left my bag somewhere else, but I couldn't have possibly done that since I was sitting down with my bag when I got my stuff out of it. Still, it was a compulsion to look around the room and try to find it. My eyes locked with Zack's during my survey of the room. He looked smugly amused. I didn't trust that look.

I was desperate to get away from the intensity of his gaze, so I did what any adult would do and slid out of my seat onto my knees below the table. Holy shit, there was my bag lying over by Zack's shoe—it must have been a size thirteen. Dare I try and peek at his crotch while under the table? For comparison, of course, to see how the size of his extremities correlate. Purely scientific reasons. *Butt fuck* that idea though. This crackerjack used his sexy long leg to reach under the table and steal my bag. That's just rude; inexcusable, really. Keeping my eyes focused on my bag—not looking at his crotch, I swear!—I crawled over and grabbed it. (My bag, not his crotch!)

It wouldn't move so I pulled on it harder, but the fucker was held firmly in place by a giant shoe sitting on its strap. I didn't want to jerk it too hard and break the strap. I quickly gave up on trying to pry it out from under that enormous clodhopper. He had to feel me pulling on the bag and he didn't even move his foot. What a *bastard*. A smart person probably would've asked him politely to move his foot, but not me. Since I couldn't pull my bag out, I decided to try and push his foot off.

When I went to push his leg, it was like trying to move a mountain. *Fuck*, it didn't even budge. I don't think he even noticed I was trying to move his leg. Moving on to Plan C, I wrapped my hands around his calf. Even through his jeans I could feel his leg was solid muscle, a fact I ignored. I tightened my grip and started shaking his leg as hard as I could, determined to work it loose enough to get my bag and get the fuck out of this store.

I was not silent in my attempts to retrieve my bag. No, I was grunting and mumbling the whole time with my strenuous efforts to get Zack off the strap. But now was not the time for dirty thoughts. Since the sounds were coming from under the table, by Zack's crotch, and I was grunting stuff like, "dirty cocksucker, you'll be lucky if I don't punch you in the balls," I'm pretty sure anyone within hearing distance thought I was giving him a rather violent handjob. And of course Zack wouldn't just move his foot so I could come out from under the table. Nope, he just sat there. He was probably making faces—like he was in deep pleasure—for everyone to see. *Bastard.*

Did I really need my bag? Maybe I should've marked the bag as a loss and run out of the store. My therapist is going to love this story. Maybe I could call her and see what she thinks I should do? But my phone was in my bag and my hands were still busy trying to tear Zack's leg apart. Maybe I should've just punched him in the balls—he'd have to move then—but his reflex would probably cause his knee to jerk into my face.

I was running out of ideas (besides just tucking tail and crawling out of the store) when Zack bent down. He had the nerve to smile at me, a warm and sexy smile that *almost* made me forget he was holding my bag hostage. "Whatcha doing, Whit?" he asked with false innocence, like he didn't know he stole my handbag. His eyes darted down and he spotted my sack. "Oh, need some help there, Whit?"

Yeah, I need you to remove your foot from my bag, and can I suggest shoving it up your ass?

Before I could actually respond though, Zack had grabbed my bag and I heard it land on the table above me. At least now I could throw my shit in it and go home. This night was not turning out how I had hoped. Stupid Jayne, ending the game before I could make my move. I'm sure I would have. When I elegantly stood back up, I froze. Zack was busy putting my things in my bag. Who does that? "What in the monkey balls are you doing? I have places for everything in there; you can't just start tossing my stuff in there."

"I know. You labeled all the pockets and dividers. Relax, I can read and am putting everything where it goes," he told me. His tone was sincere and placating. And he was almost done shoving everything in so what could I really do about it? Just let him finish and then I could leave, go home and pretend this night never happened. He finished packing away my stuff and looked up at me with those sweet puppy eyes that he could have probably used to get away with murder just by flashing them. "You ready?" he asked quietly. I nodded before I even thought about it, mesmerized by those peepers. Using his eyes like a weapon seemed like a dirty play. *Manipulative bastard.*

With that, he grabbed my bag and headed for the door. I had to follow; he had my stuff after all. So I trailed behind him, walking across the parking lot. I watched as he opened the back door of his car and tossed my bag on the seat. What the fuck was he doing? "Get in," Zack said as he opened the driver's door. I just stared at him; he couldn't expect me to get in the car with him, could he? "Hurry up, I'm starving. I'll take you to dinner. We need to talk strategy for next week's game."

I don't know what I was thinking, but I found myself slowly getting into his car. I may have been in some kind of daze, because he was pulling out of the lot before I even managed to get my seatbelt buckled. I'm not sure how long we sat in silence before he casually asked, "Why did your mom name you Whitney?"

I must have been really stunned by his question because I found myself responding before I even thought about it. "She thought she was going to have a baby girl because she craved cucumbers and seafood during her second trimester. Apparently those are girl foods. Anyway, when she was wrong and had me, she didn't want to have to think of a boy name so went with what she planned to name a girl."

"But you said her name was Whitney?"

"Yeah, she says she knew she'd be the coolest mom ever and that her and her kid would be best friends, so she wanted to have the same name. Apparently, having the same name increases the mother and child's ability to bond." I wasn't embarrassed by my name, I just preferred Whit. That way if I was hanging out with my mom, I wouldn't get confused which one of us people were talking about.

"Is she a cool mom?"

"The coolest," I responded. After a few minutes with Zack not saying anything, I found myself spilling more words without thinking. "You know I only got in the car because you were holding my bag hostage." *And because you're so fucking hot, I want to lean over and wrap my lips around your cock until you shoot down my throat.* Yeah, I wanted my dessert before dinner, and right fucking then would have been preferred. Luckily, I didn't say that part out loud.

"That doesn't sound very romantic, now does it?" he asked, glancing my way for a second before looking back at the road. "Look at it this way: I was being a gentleman; I carried your books for you, offered you a ride, and now I'm taking you out to dinner. Dare I say it sounds almost like I'm trying to woo you?" He finished by turning his head and giving me a quick wink.

If I thought he was serious, I would have told him to consider me wooed before I started pulling down his zipper using my teeth. But since he said he wanted to talk strategy, I was pretty sure he was just yanking my chain. If he was serious, he would have made a move by now, right?

But I was seriously into him and I hadn't made a move. Maybe he was just really horny and didn't want to waste time finding a hook-up. That brought some dirty thoughts to mind.

I must have been really into my fantasy world, because before I knew it, I was following Zack into a twenty-four hour diner I'd never been to before. We were seated quickly in a booth along the wall. It looked like a typical diner, a little worn but cozy. At first, I thought if he was trying to woo me, he wasn't trying very hard, but then I considered where we just came from and what we were wearing, and the place seemed perfect.

Shortly after being seated, a young server brought menus and water, and introduced herself as Lindsey. After taking our drink order, she left us with time to look at the menu. I got a mint chip milkshake—my favorite—so that way if I didn't get sex with Zack later, at least the night wouldn't be completely unsatisfying. Yes, I loved mint chip shakes that much. Zack got an iced tea, no lemon; it seemed like a boring drink to me.

We hadn't spoken since the car ride here. It was okay not talking in the car because I was daydreaming, and right now I was hiding behind my menu. But that only lasted a few minutes, up until Lindsey came back with the drinks and to take our orders. I ordered two cheesy baked potatoes. I wasn't that hungry and I loved potatoes and cheese, my two favorite foods which together were heavenly. Zack ordered a heart attack on a platter. Then Lindsey left, taking my menu shield with her.

Zack sat there silently looking at me. I was used to this; my therapist often played the same game. I think she called it "stare at the nut until he cracks and starts spilling his guts." I always lost at this game so I knew I'd have to speak first. I went with the only thing I could think of. "Why did you join our RPG group?" I sounded harsh even to my own ears, like he'd done something wrong and I was interrogating him. "That came out wrong. What I meant was what made you want to start role playing?" That sounded much better.

"Well it's kind of a long story, but a few weeks before I joined the group, I broke up with my boyfriend. And I kind of spent those three weeks bitching to my friend Chandra non-stop about how I always date idiot losers. She tried to tell me it's because I always went for the same type of guy who I'd meet at a club or party. I told her she was wrong and I just had bad luck with men." He paused to take a sip of his tea. I was trying to suck my thick shake through the narrow straw. "Anyway, we were having a drink at a café and saw Jayne's flyer looking for new members for a Tuesday and Thursday night RPG group. I guess Chandra was completely fed up with my whining because she bet I couldn't last two weeks with a group outside of my normal social setting. I didn't want her to think I couldn't do it, so I emailed Jayne and you know the rest. After the two weeks, I won fifty bucks."

"How kind of you to grace us with your presence, but in case you can't tell time, two weeks passed awhile ago." I know I sounded bitter, but it ticked me off he thought we were below his standards when he had to be cock and balled into joining our group and had planned to leave after two weeks. It took two weeks just to get him ready to start playing the game. I'd have been so pissed if he had just stopped showing up after that.

"Well, Chandra was right. I did need to broaden my social activities. At first I was a little bored with all the character development and learning the rules, but once we started playing I really began to love it." He sounded sincere, and he hadn't missed a game yet, but still…

"Why do you love it?" I wasn't being antagonistic; I really wanted to know why he loved it.

He just smiled at me for a few long seconds. "Because I get to say whatever I want when I'm in the game. Sapphire doesn't hold back, she says what's on her mind. I work with a lot of sucktards and wish I could say half the stuff to them I get to say when we play. I guess the game is like a release for me, where I get to let everything out of my system. It's like therapy."

"Trust me, it's better than therapy." He gave me one of his trademarked eyebrow raises at my statement. I shrugged. I'm not going to tell him about my therapy sessions.

"There was another reason I stayed and why I keep coming back." He smiled coyly at me. I used my hand to motion for him to continue but he just smiled at me.

He was going to be a douche and make me ask, wasn't he? "And what's that?"

"There is this really cute guy on the team I wanted to get to know better." He was still smiling, and even though he just admitted he liked someone else, that smile made me ache in my jeans.

"Randy?" I asked. I had to know who he thought was cute. "I guess he is kind of cute if he doesn't talk."

"Randy? Are you serious?" He looked a little repulsed. "Have you seen Randy picking stuff out of his hair and sniffing it? It's totally gross."

"Bre—"

"Don't say Brett, moron." I would've been snarky about him cutting me off or calling me a moron, except he said it so affectionately, like a pet name. "I'm talking about you."

"Me? Why me?"

"Why you? Because I think you're gorgeous, and I adore the way you think you're shy, but you're really not, you just think too much. The first time I saw you, I forgot to breathe. Then when you looked at me with those big green eyes, I got lost and knew I needed to get to know you better."

"If you wanted to get to know me better, why'd you wait until now to kidnap me?" I asked cheekily as I smiled probably the biggest smile of my life upon hearing him describe me.

"It's difficult to 'kidnap' someone, as you say, when you can't get them alone. You always rush out after the games and I never had a chance to talk to you. And honestly, I'm used to the other guy making the first move. I've never had to plan a seduction before."

"This is what you call a seduction?"

He laughed and shook his head, "The real planning comes into play later."

"Judging by how you asked me out, I can only imagine how dirty you play."

"You'll have to wait and see," he smirked at me. "But until then I really do need you to help me figure out how Sapphire will escape before, you know, they rape her sexy ass or some shit like that."

How could I point out—without being a dick—that she doesn't have the skill to escape? "What is your character the best at?"

"Talking shit!" he answered immediately. I couldn't help but laugh. Fuck me, he was cute. And he made me smile like no one else ever had.

"Okay, what's the second thing she's the best at?" I asked when I stopped laughing.

"Healing shit?"

"Bingo, every time it's your turn, all you have to do is regenerate. Keep your health points full, and when Cable comes to rescue you, you'll be ready to go," I told him, outlining the only logical thing to do in his position. "And you won't get raped. The Draczards are androgynous."

"That's bullshit, Whit. You expect Ms. Sapphire to just sit there and wait for a man to come save her? She doesn't need a man. Just help me come up with my own escape plan." His ambition was cute but he really didn't get how the game worked.

"Look, you can't escape. Just not possible; you don't have the right character skills for it. It will be a while before Cable rescues Sapphire. Jayne has some evil plan. She takes Game Master duties seriously, and kidnapping Sapphire was meant to be a distraction. She thinks I'll go save you before finishing the quest, but by the time you're rescued she'll already have done what she has planned. So I need to finish the quest and then go save you. And while I'm doing that, all you have to do is stay alive, so keep regenerating health." There it was, all laid out. He couldn't argue with that, right? I mean it was so obviously the only way to handle this situation.

"That is a sucky plan. I have to just sit there and heal myself repeatedly while you're off having an adventure?"

"Well, you can still belittle your captors, and try to wear them down to such a state of depression they'll release you because they can't handle your verbal onslaught any longer," I said with a little smile. I thought he'd like being able to sit there and toss insults until his voice turned hoarse.

"That sounds more tolerable, but I still want to be out exploring, not tied to a cement slab in some lizard freak's sex dungeon." By 'exploring' he meant his obsessive need to have Sapphire pick every herb we saw and open every crate looking for unneeded treasure. Sometimes when I was playing, I'd picture Cable pushing the little gnome into the crate, closing it, and carrying it off. It would decrease the travel time not having to wait while Sapphire stopped every few squares to interact with her surroundings. Maybe if Cable had locked her in a crate the kidnappers wouldn't have found her and she wouldn't be messing up the quest.

I was saved from having to respond to Zack by the arrival of our food. This was a good thing since I didn't know what to say. We were eating in silence when Zack randomly asked, "Want a fry?" I thought about it for a second. I mean I was eating two potatoes as it was, but the gesture seemed sweet. And wasn't sharing food supposed to be romantic?

I nodded my head as he picked up a fry, dunked it in mayonnaise, and then shoved it in my mouth. I hate mayonnaise but couldn't spit it out since he was still pushing the fry in. I was expecting him to offer me his plate and let me grab it. He hadn't washed his hands for hours; at least I rubbed some sanitizer on mine right after we sat down. Not that I'm germ-phobic or anything. Hell, I'd lick every part of Zack except his hands or feet. Was that weird, 'feel free to choke me with your cock, but keep your fingers away from my lips?' I'll be the first to admit it makes no sense, but in my head I couldn't get over those fingers near my mouth. It was gross.

It would be rude to grab his wrist and spit the food out, but I still considered it an option. I'm pretty sure he'd be repulsed if I spit the slightly chewed fry out and scrubbed my tongue clean on a napkin. The only thing I could do was get through it with the thought that if I survived this, later he'd hopefully stuff my mouth with his cock. I closed my lips tightly on the end of the fry; no way was I letting his fingers get inside my mouth. After I swallowed the last of the fry, I opened my eyes. Zack was grinning at me. I tried to smile back without parting my lips. It felt awkward, so I imagine I looked sick or something. If he said anything I'd say it was because he made my stomach flutter.

"You have some mayo on your lips," he said, reaching out and brushing the corner of my mouth with his thumb. I almost gasped but managed to keep my lips closed. I turned my head and grabbed my napkin and quickly wiped at my face before downing my full glass of water. It didn't help the memory and the taste still lingered. I'd likely never forget this; my therapist would probably make me relive it for at least three sessions, the sadistic bitch.

"Thanks," I mumbled, trying not to look queasy as I turned back to him. "Want some of my shake?" I asked, trying to be polite even though I was still trying to get over the mayo-assault on my taste buds. As first dates went, it could be worse. At least I'm pretty sure this was a date. At his nod, I passed him my almost empty milkshake. I almost had a spontaneous orgasm when he wrapped his full lips around the straw and started sucking. He licked his bottom lip after releasing the straw. I was suddenly feeling jealous of that straw.

He passed my drink back and grabbed another fry, dunking it in his fat sauce. "Want another fry?" he asked smoothly. I knew I had two choices here: accept the fry, and then have him try and shove food in my mouth every time we ate together, or say no thanks and explain myself. Of course there was only one real option. I had to tell him to keep his fingers away from my face or I'd always worry he might try to touch my lips again.

"No fry for me, thanks. I hate mayonnaise, and I freak out a bit having hands near my mouth and nose." I tried to sound casual even as the memory of his thumb caressing my lip made me itch to go scrub my face clean.

"Oh shit, I'm sorry. It didn't cross my mind that you might not like mayo." He sounded so apologetic I *almost* thought about lying and saying, "I love mayonnaise and hands touching my mouth."

"Guess I'll have to remember to keep my hands away from your face."

"Well I have no problems with your hands anywhere else, like in my hair," I winked at him, hoping to revamp the mood. "And you can still feed me; just don't use your fingers."

"Oh yeah, you like having a fist pulling your hair?" I could hear the excitement in his voice at the idea.

"You'll have to wait and see," I said nonchalantly, replaying his words from earlier back to him.

"Looks like we're done here, so want to come over to my place and play a game?" As creepy as that offer could have sounded, his tone was seductive and not at all like the psychotic voice from the movie *Saw*. I watched it in the theater back when I was in high school, and I screamed like a drowning duck. There were little girls there who didn't scream as much as I did. Needless to say, I didn't watch the sequels.

"We just got done playing a game. Why would you want to play another?" I asked stupidly. He was inviting me to his place. Why the fuck did I care what his reason was? I should've just said, "Yes, please I'd love to."

"Well I was thinking of playing a more active game, something to get our blood pumping. Maybe Strip Twister or Nude Wii Tennis, or we could just watch a movie if you prefer."

"Don't you need at least three people to play Twister? You know, someone to spin and call out colors while the rest act like uncoordinated monkeys." I could have slapped myself right then for again being dense. The correct response was, 'Let's play Naked Anything for hours, please.' "Yeah, another game or movie would be fun. We should do that." Could my response have seemed any more robotic?

Zack paid and we headed out to his car. The ride to his place was spent with Zack talking about his car, or maybe cars in general. I couldn't really follow along but I enjoyed listening to his voice, even if he might as well have been speaking German for all I understood. Before long we were pulling up to his building and he was leading me through a nice but plain lobby into the elevator. Disappointingly, nothing happened in the elevator. Probably for the best since there was an older couple in the metal box with us and they probably wouldn't know what to make of my attempt at flirting. They'd freak out thinking I was having a seizure or something, and it's not nice to scare the elderly.

The elevator opened on the fifth floor and Zack led me down the hall. I watched his ass thinking I'd follow that anywhere. *Fucking Hawt.* Watching his ass flex as he walked motivated me more to work up the courage to get touchy-flirty, because I needed to get a good view of that ass without clothes. Then we were at his door and he was motioning me inside.

I'm going to skip the boring details, like what his apartment looked like, because honestly, who even notices those details when they're hornier than a bunny on ecstasy and alone with a God-like Zack? So yeah, his home has walls with stuff in frames hanging, but more importantly, where was the bedroom? *Fuck*, he had a nice muscular ass. Bet he had impeccable control with those hips. Why were we still clothed and standing in the entryway? Why wasn't he going caveman and shredding my clothes on the way to his room? I was nervous and my thoughts had become jumpy. "Did you want something to drink?" he asked as he walked further into his condo.

"No drink. Didn't you mention something about a seduction plan and stripping?" Right to the point, but I'd been hard for hours and maintaining an erection that long messes with a man's blood circulation to other areas, like the filter for his mouth.

Zack turned around and gave me a small smile. "About that, I lied earlier. I have no plan and thought I could make up something as we went. I wanted you and couldn't wait anymore. Watching you play earlier, it was captivating. I love how into the game you get; you play with your whole body, and watching you is always so intense. I've been dying to see if that intensity would transfer over to more intimate activities." He gave a sly grin. "And you're the best storyteller, the way you keep the story going even as you roll the dice, or how quick you are to react to the other players. I can't help but wonder what you'd say during sex… do you talk dirty?"

Oh, fuck me with a basketball, he'd been thinking of me *and* sex? Thinking leads to expectations, which can lead to disappointments, which added so much pressure to perform well. I mean, I wanted to fuck him like an all-star anyway so he'd want repeat performances. Dirty talk, though? Not sure I could pull that off. There was a fine line between 'dirty hot' and 'dirty gross.' I'd probably be 'dirty gross,' or worse, 'dirty boring.'

"We don't have to have to sex on the first date, but you did seem open to the idea at the diner. We could just watch a movie or something. Up to you." Oh shit in a bucket, now he thinks my hesitation is because I'm not interested.

I needed to think quickly to show I was very interested but not seem too desperate. "I would have let you fuck me in the backseat, before dinner even." *Mission: Don't Seem Slutty.* Fail. Try again. "It doesn't really count as a date if you blackmailed the person into going on said date." Oh dear lord, I needed to just shut the fuck up and stop talking. *You've wanted to go on a date with him for months; don't play coy now. Who cares how he asked you out, just get to the sex.* "I'm not one of those queens that have a stupid sex rule, like three dates first. Even if I did, I'd break it for you," I said in what I hoped was a teasingly seductive manner. That was kind of smooth… a little slutty, a little sweet. Let's be honest: I'm no saint and currently hornier than fuck. "If it feels right, why not just do it?"

"In the backseat? Damn, if I'd known you were that easy, well… I still would have wanted to eat first," he whispered in my ear. When'd he get so close? I could feel his warm breath against my cheek. I could easily turn my head and kiss him. And I wanted to kiss him badly, so I did. A gentle brush of lips, at first, quickly turned into a hard mashing of lips that couldn't get close enough and a tangling of tongues as they sensually caressed against each other. The way Zack kissed me was mind-blowing, or maybe I blacked out for a moment. One minute I was standing there moaning into Zack's kiss, and the next I was laying on the hardwood floor, Zack still ravaging my mouth, his body pressing on top of mine. I had my legs wrapped around his waist, our cocks rubbing against each other. We were still clothed, unfortunately.

I was dazed and my only thought was getting Zack naked—and hopefully inside me—and the quickest way to get what I wanted was to demand it. "Naked, now!" I growl-moaned as I pulled out of the kiss. It might not have been the most complete sentence but I knew he got the message when he stood up, forcing me to unwrap my legs from around his waist. He reached out his hand and helped me up. I wobbled for a couple of seconds like a drunken penguin. Zack helped to steady me before grabbing my hand and jerking me behind him, I assumed towards the bedroom or someplace more comfortable to ravage each other.

I was right. He led me into the bedroom. I'm sure it was nice but all I noticed was the large sleigh bed. It had a wood frame with drawers on the bottom, and the mattress had to be three feet off the floor. My mind immediately went to all the wonderful things we could do on that bed, but where to start? It would probably be best to start with Zack, but where was he, and why wasn't he touching me and ripping my clothes apart? I quickly scanned the room and saw Zack kneeling down and rummaging around inside his closet. I walked to him and looked over his shoulder to see what was more important than getting sweaty and naked. *Holy Fucking Draczard!* He had a *huge* cardboard box of condoms in his closet. I was so busy staring at the box trying to guestimate how many condoms were in there, I didn't notice Zack stand up until he spoke. "Okay, I got the supplies. Let's get back to what we were doing."

As I looked at him, I think my eyes widened to the point they were about to pop out of my head. He was grinning seductively at me while standing there, holding a strip of condoms and what was probably a gallon of lube. "*Holy Fucking Caterpillars*, that is a massive bottle of lube! Do you run a sex club or something?" My voice sounded a little higher pitched than usual, but I was a little freaked out. Safe sex supplies in those quantities were for sex-experts and I'm sex-average at best. I could take cock like a man, but I was neither a sexcrobat nor sexually innovative.

"A sex club? What are you talking about?"

"You have a jug of lube and a box of condoms in your closet." I paused, thinking that sounded too ordinary. "Well, I have a box of six condoms in my nightstand. What you have is a crate of... what? A thousand condoms in your closet?"

"I buy in bulk, the little lube bottle is empty, and I'm in a hurry and don't want to fill it up. Can we talk about this after we fuck? Because

I'm having trouble focusing on anything other than the need to fuck you." Oh that sounded like a good idea, much better than continuing on with thoughts that were just making me develop performance anxiety. If we were RPG characters, his sex skill level would be in the fifties while mine was still in the single digits. Thoughts like that just weren't helping so I decided to clear my head and enjoy the night.

And enjoy the night I would. I mean just seeing Zack naked was a guarantee for a fantastic night. Anything else was just 'raspberries on top' as mom would say.

I think I might have had an inner ear infection or vertigo or something, because one minute I'm standing there watching Zack carrying a strip of condoms and an army-sized bucket of lube towards his nightstand. Then the next thing I know I'm naked and flat on my back in the center of the bed with an equally naked Zack on top of me.

He positioned his cock so it was above my mouth while his face was above my groin. His cock was on the large side and my lips could barely stretch around it. I used my tongue and lips to tease around the head. It'd be a while before I'd be able to deep throat his cock, but I'm pretty sure he enjoyed what I was able to do, judging by the noises he made as he sucked my cock. His mouth was incredible; he closed his lips tightly around me as he worked up and down the shaft. I had to focus on pleasing him or I'd come way too quickly.

I pulled the thick head of his cock out of my mouth and slowly worked my lips and tongue down his long shaft. I gently used the tip of my tongue to lightly tease his large, low-hanging balls. I brought my hand up and started stroking his cock as I pulled one of his balls into my mouth. After a few minutes I started to pull my mouth away, letting his ball slowly slip out from between my lips. I moved to his other one, giving it the same treatment as I tightened my hand and started to stroke his cock faster.

I'd gotten into a steady rhythm of tonguing his balls while jerking his cock. It was a snug fit but I'd managed to get both of his balls in my mouth and was stimulating them with my tongue. I loved the salty flavor and his manly musk scent.

I was so into working his hard cock and balls I almost didn't notice when he pulled off me, until he started moaning louder, "Oh fuck, keep sucking my nuts while you fist-fuck my cock." His words increased my need to make him come. I started sucking on his balls harder and turning my wrist a little when I reached the head of his cock, making my thumb caress the sensitive skin underneath. I knew he liked that when, on the second upstroke, he shouted, "Sweet Jesus, I'm coming," before I felt his body tense as his cock erupted above me. I felt the first strand of his come land on my chest and stomach, followed by another jet that landed on my upper chest. The rest of his man ranch dribbled out to pool in the hollow of my neck. I continued pumping his cock until he grabbed my arm and made me stop. I knew he was most likely too sensitive but I loved the feeling of his hard cock in my hand.

I let his tasty balls slip out of my mouth and forced myself to let go of his cock. As soon as I removed my hand, his warm mouth enveloped my prick. I didn't even know how close I was to orgasm until his moist tongue started teasing the tip of my cock, pressing against the slit. I barely had time to whimper, "I'm coming," before I released my load in his mouth. He swallowed every drop and made sure I was spiffy clean before letting my spent cock slip free.

He turned around and flopped on the bed so we were on our backs next to each other. I dragged my hands up my stomach and felt the come that had landed there. Being overly relaxed, commonly known as lazy, I didn't want to get up but I didn't want it to start dripping either, so I did the only logical thing: I rubbed it into my skin. The large amount of come on my neck had already started running down both sides. I've read a few articles that talk about how healthy come is for hair and skin; now was my chance to try it for myself. I just had to remember to shower before Zack drove me back to my car.

Rubbing the come against my skin left my hands sticky so I tried to covertly wipe them off on the corner of Zack's bed sheet. If he noticed what I was doing, he didn't say. We both lay there. I was just staring at the ceiling, feeling satisfied. I wasn't sure how long we stayed there before Zack broke the silence. "There were ten thousand condoms in that box." He sounded so relaxed and casual, like everyone had ten thousand condoms and gallon-sized containers of lube. I was so sated that it took me a minute to process what he'd said.

Turning my head to look at him, I asked, "Why do you need so many condoms? I know I'm not an expert, but ten thousand seems excessive." Or was I just inadequate with my box of only six? I guess it'd been awhile since I last had sex, but surely not that much had changed in eight months, right? I think I would have heard about any big changes in sexual practices, even if I wasn't practicing too often.

"Well I might've been a little presumptuous and thought I'd ordered one hundred of them. Then I received a box of ten thousand fuck wrappers. I'm still not sure how I fucked up the order." He paused to grab a condom off the nightstand and tossed it on my chest. "And I can only use them with you," he winked. I grabbed the condom off my chest and actually looked at it for the first time. The wrapper had a longsword going diagonally across the condom. The handle was in the bottom right corner with the tip of the blade ending in the top left corner. There was a semi-translucent black condom being unrolled down the sword. It stopped a little below the tip. "**EVEN A BADASS WARRIOR NEEDS TO SHEATH HIS LONGSWORD**" was written in tiny block print across the middle of the wrapper.

At first, I thought it was weird ordering so many custom condoms, but then I realized what a sweet gesture it was. I mean, that takes a lot of thought and planning. It was the sweetest thing anyone had ever done for me. I wasn't sure what to say. 'Thank you, you're very sweet' seemed lame. I wanted to say something sweet and heartfelt to convey how much his unexpected gesture meant to me. "Wow, that must have cost a small fortune." *Mission: Be Romantic* was an EPIC FAIL! I might as well have just said, "Thanks for the gift, how much did it cost, and can I return it for cash?"

I was frantically trying to think of something to say that would distract from what I just said when Zack responded, "To do what we just did, it was totally worth it."

"We haven't even used one yet."

"I know. And it was already more than worth it."

"It will take a lot of sex to go through ten thousand condoms." I wondered if my voice sounded as awed as I felt. I was still trying to wrap my head around this.

"Yeah, and we only have two years before they expire." Zack sounded like he was bragging, meanwhile I was busy trying to do the math for how many condoms we needed to use a day.

"That means we have to use like thirteen and a half a day." I took a minute to process that. "Which isn't possible so we will have to rotate and use thirteen one day and fourteen the next. That seems like a lot of work and logistically not probable. I mean with other stuff happening, something could come up or one of us get sick, and then we have to try and get caught back up." The thought of fucking so much was hot but kind of exhausting. And we'd have to work out a sex-schedule and then it would really feel like work.

"Just means you'll be too busy to have sex with anyone else. I don't see a problem with that." He paused for a moment. "And I already used over 400 of them. We'll just have to get condom creative. Have water condom-balloon fights and stuff. So yeah, we'll have tons of fun fucking like crazy and using condoms for weird shit."

"What? How did you use four hundred already?"

"I'm working on a collage and it needs four hundred, but I got carried away with the hot glue gun and burned holes through some of them. It's still a work in progress."

"So you're a sexy artist?"

"Sexy, yes. Artist, no. I went to a website for making collages. You know, you upload the photos you're working with, and the image you want to make with them, and how big you want it to be. I wanted to make a giant condom wrapper, so it is twenty condoms wide and twenty high. I wanted the image to look like a giant version of the custom condoms. Turns out you have to have different images to blend the colors together, so instead of a real collage I have a fifty-square-inch square that will have four hundred condoms hot glued on it."

"It still sounds awesome. I can't wait to see it. What are you going to do with it when it's done?" I asked curiously.

"Originally I planned to impress you with it. I was hoping when you saw it you'd be all, like, wooed and then I'd say something like, 'I want to stick my big sword in your tight sheath,' and you'd be so enamored by the collage you wouldn't notice how corny I am," he said, grinning at me like a cheeseball. (Some people say goofball, but I like cheese and balls, and I really like Zack's balls.)

"All you had to do was show me your sword and I'd be more than impressed and let you sheath it wherever you wanted," I replied, proud of myself for being flirty and not saying something like, "I like corn," which I do, but that doesn't sound sexy (unless you have a food fetish).

"I know that now. The collage idea was before I knew how easy you were," he said teasingly. I was still thinking about corn.

"Hey, Zack, you have a food fetish?" I asked because it was best to know these things, especially since I'd committed to having lots and lots of sex with him.

"Not particularly, but I like food, so if you have a food fetish, it's cool." Damn his voice was sexy.

"I don't either. I was just thinking about corn." I hoped he didn't ask me why I was thinking about it, because I seriously didn't know.

He rolled over, hovering above me, and put his lips by my ear, "I never had a boyfriend that got excited about corn before."

"I don't get turned on thinking about corn. And who said I'd be your boyfriend?" I moaned when he lowered his body to rub against mine.

"You feel excited and you said you were thinking about corn. And you have to be my boyfriend; I'm making you condom art."

"Trust me, it's not the corn that's making me hard, and you are persuasive with your mating rituals. Stealing, blackmail, weird art gifts, and really great sex... who could say no to that?"

"When you put it like that it sounds like the best first date ever. Now shut up so we can get started on using these condoms." That sounded like a brilliant idea. Not that conversation was possible since he'd barely finished his sentence before his lips were sealed to mine. Then he pulled away again to whisper, "Don't forget I want to hear you talk dirty."

****

Later that night...
Mission: Dirty Play. EPIC SUCCESS!

THE END

Dirty Drag

Copyright© 2013 Kyle Adams

It Begins In an Alley

"Motherfucker!" Ashley yelled as he stubbed his toe against whatever was carelessly discarded in the alley. It was too dark to see anything, even using his cell phone screen as a poor imitation flashlight. It was his third time walking through this alley. He knew the door was here somewhere; he'd spent hours researching on the internet for the perfect dive bar for tonight's experiment. If only his research warned him to bring a searchlight to navigate through the musty alley. A nose plug wouldn't have been a bad idea either, so he wouldn't have to keep his nose pinched between his fingers to avoid the putrid smells of rotting trash and stale piss. *Classy*.

The small pub didn't have any signs, and the only entrance was an old steel door down a dark passage. Cliché as it was, Ashley wasn't too worried about being stabbed by an unknown assailant lurking in the shadows; he was armed with a can of pepper spray and could scream like a banshee. If he didn't find that damn door soon, he'd know every fucking pothole, rock, or piece of garbage cluttering the alleyway. Over ten minutes of searching and not a single person had come or gone from the bar. Ashley was going to find that fucking door, even if it took all night. He needed to go somewhere he wouldn't be recognized, and no one he knew would be caught dead in this shit hole. Fuck, after this he'd probably have to go home and burn his outfit for sanitary reasons before scrubbing his skin raw in a scorching shower.

Finally finding the door five minutes later, Ashley tried to pull it open, but it was heavier than he expected and didn't budge. He heaved as hard as he could the second time; the door still didn't fucking move. Ashley held the grimy door handle with both hands, and braced himself with his stylish, but affordable, stiletto heel against the wall. He was going to rip this heavier-than-fuck door off its fucking hinges if he had to. It was too dark out to worry about anyone seeing how he looked with his mini skirt rising up, ass exposed and high heel flat against the building.

Adjusting his grip on the handle, he was a second away from jerking back full force when he felt the door swing inward. Ashley fell forward with the door and stumbled from the surprise. He almost fell into the short man that had opened the door. If not for the numerous experiences he had walking in heels while drunk off his ass, Ashley would have snapped one of those four-inch heels and fallen right into the little man. Ashley liked his men bigger than his own five feet and eleven inches, or six feet, three inches with these heels on. He was glad he caught himself before the little guy could try and cop a feel. He was feeling a little foolish that he never thought to try and push the door open. Wasn't it required by fire code for doors to open outward? Probably also code to have a well lit and clear entrance/exit path, but obviously this place was *too fancy* to bother with customer safety or city regulations.

"Watch it, Amazonian," Tiny snapped, as he brushed by Ashley, pushing him so the door bumped into his ass. *What a* jerk, Ashley thought. After all, the little ogre was the one who jerked the door open in the first place.

"Well excuse me, Mr. McShorty Tiny-Dick, I must have overlooked that you were there. I'm sure you're used to it."

"Stupid bitch," Tiny said, as he disappeared into the alley.

Not one to let someone walk away with the last word, Ashley shouted, "What's wrong, you scared of a real woman?" The irony of his statement wasn't missed, and he hoped his voice didn't give away that he, in fact, was not a real woman; just a man in a skirt. Ashley thought he'd be lucky to make it through tonight without getting his ass kicked, but he never did know when to bite his tongue. And if anyone started shit, he wasn't about to just bend over and take it; he'd throw shit right back at them and hope for the best and that things didn't turn physical. He bruised too easily.

Pulling his skirt back down and taking a deep breath, Ashley turned and walked into the bar. He looked around, but no one was showing him any interest. He knew they'd probably heard his yelling, but he was glad to see they didn't care. It was probably a normal thing here, people yelling and hurling insults. His altercation with Tiny not causing any extra scrutiny would certainly make the night easier; he didn't need people looking at him too closely. If anyone noticed he wasn't a real woman, he'd be fortunate if they only kicked his ass. Ashley was confident however, that no one would catch on to the fact he was really a man. He spent hours getting ready for this and was positive he could pull it off; he even perfected his squeaky bimbo voice and had been practicing his airhead giggle for weeks.

He rarely did drag but certainly enjoyed it on occasion. Mostly, he liked wearing high heels and wore them any chance he got. It was a lot of work doing full drag. Ashley was lucky to have natural curves and a shapely ass, so he didn't need to worry about padding around the hips. It was easy for him to stuff a small, B cup bra and use a little makeup to silhouette his chest, making it appear like he had a luscious rack. The hair was easy, throw on his favorite wig and style it a little if needed. Ashley preferred not to think about the unpleasantness that was *dick tucking*; tucking was a painful bitch. It's not easy being a queen.

Tonight was about proving he could pass for a real woman. Ashley thought back to a few weeks ago, when he went out with some friends while in drag. His friend, Jared, kept saying he would never be able to pass as a woman, but that didn't stop him from trying to feel up under Ashley's skirt. Ashley had made it clear he needed a man, one who was big and capable of holding him down and wasn't afraid of fucking him good and hard; a man who wasn't intimidated by Ashley's height when he wore high-heels.

At the time, Ashley said it wasn't about looking like a real woman but about how he felt when he dressed up as one. Which was total bullshit; all Ashley really wanted was to wear the high heels out dancing. But, no one would understand that. His gay friends were fine with him dressing in drag, but if he simply wore high heels while dressed as a man, they would ask all kinds of questions and act like he was a freak for having a fetish for wearing woman's shoes.

So, by the end of tonight, he was going to prove Jared wrong, or so he hoped. Moving forward with his plan, he walked up to the bar and ordered a drink. Thankfully, the bartender didn't ask for any identification or he would have had to come up with some excuse for how he must have left it somewhere. Ashley picked up his drink and headed for a booth along the wall where the bar's weak lighting was even lower. The dim light would make it harder for anyone to notice anything odd about him, like that he had a penis tucked between his legs, for example, but it would also make it harder for him to check his makeup.

****

Rick sat at the bar, facing the door, drinking his beer. He subtly watched as the pretty little redhead adjusted the short skirt before strutting up to the bar. *Well, not so little*, he thought to himself. Wearing those come-fuck-me heels, Gorgeous was probably just a couple inches shorter than Rick. The shoes were black with pointed open toes. Rick could see those sexy toes were painted the same deep red as the hair flowing down to broad shoulders. If Rick hadn't already noticed an Adam's apple, he would have known it was a man from those muscular shoulders alone; women just didn't have shoulders like that. Of course, no straight man would notice those things either, because they would be staring at that chest. Wearing a skin tight, low cut, black top with a padded bra and chest makeup; it looked like he was stacked. Rick had to examine closely to make sure the guy didn't have implants, his chest looked so real.

Rick watched as he took his drink over to a booth in the shadows along the back wall. Such a fine ass barely covered by the black leather miniskirt. An ass Rick wanted to get to know better. And those legs, damn Rick was hard just imagining those legs wrapped around his waist. The high heels made his shapely muscles stand out as they flowed up into his perfect ass. Rick first noticed two things about a person: a fine ass and a personality. One without the other just didn't work for him. He already noticed that tight, round ass came with a spitfire personality.

Rick had had trouble not bursting out into laughter when this beautiful looking woman laid into that asshole, Ronald. Then he just sauntered up to the bar, like metaphorically castrating assholes was an everyday experience. Well, maybe it was for this guy. All Rick knew was that, as soon as he saw that fine ass, he knew he'd have to find out if this sexy stranger was just as spunky between the sheets.

Rick patiently observed as the man sat down and pulled a mirror and some makeup out of a tiny red purse. Rick knew it was Sexy's first time at Sal's just by the way he looked around when he first stumbled in after the Ronald incident. Rick figured it would be best to give him time to settle in before he made his move. He had been coming to Sal's bar for a few years now, ever since a coworker brought him here after work, and he knew it could take some getting used to. Sal's got a lot of new patrons every night. It had a reputation for being a shady dive bar where one could find almost anything they were looking for and even a few things they weren't. So, each night, people would show up looking to score something, only to find out that what they heard about Sal's was wrong, then leave disappointed, never to venture down to Sal's again. Or, like Rick, they loved the laid-back atmosphere and enjoyed relaxing after work with reasonably priced drinks and cheap fried food.

In the years that he had been coming here, he never once saw anyone remotely as attractive as the pretty thing sitting in the back booth making faces at his compact mirror. He was pinching his plump lips together and making what Rick could only describe as fish faces. He was probably trying to make sure his lipstick was still perfect and not needing a touch up. Rick almost missed it, he wasn't the best lip reader, but he was pretty sure those lips mouthed, "I'd fuck me," and Rick couldn't agree more with that statement. His hard cock pressing against the seam of his jeans was a constant reminder of just how much he wanted to bury himself in that ass.

After Sexy finished talking into the mirror, he focused on his eye shadow and alternately wiggled both brows while heavily concentrating on his reflection. When he seemed reassured that his face was still gorgeous, he set the mirror upright on the table. Looking down into it, he adjusted his bra, holding both hands under his fake breasts and fiddling with each of them. Someone really should let him know his chest already looked fine. Once satisfied that they weren't uneven or lumpy, he closed the mirror and put everything back into his purse.

Rick was wondering how much time he should wait before introducing himself. His cock was pretty insistent that he'd waited more than long enough. Another guy approached the table first, but Rick didn't mind. Competition would make the reward that much sweeter. And he couldn't really be surprised that he wasn't the only one to notice someone that hot walk in here. It was pretty rare for a woman to come in here alone, and even more uncommon for it to be one looking that sexy. So, Rick sat back, sipped his drink, and waited patiently to see how this would play out.

****

Ashley had finished putting away his beauty kit after confirming he still looked flawless. He was about to enjoy his drink when Redneck Joe walked up in his blue plaid lumber jacket, tooth pick dangling between his lips, and, by way of greeting, drawled, "Your tits looked bigger from a distance." RJ stopped to scratch his scalp under his plain trucker hat, "But guess you'll still do."

Of course his tits looked smaller when looking down his shirt. The makeup-illusion only worked when looking mostly straight at his chest. Ashley tried to push his chest out but there was only so much boobage he could get wearing a B-cup bra. And, he was proud of his little boobs; big ones just got in the way and encouraged fondling. "Um thanks, but I'll have to pass on whatever it was I'd still do for," Ashley said, in his most vapid voice. Ashley wanted to simply tell him to "fuck off," but he was pleased this hillbilly thought he was a biological woman, so he let it slide.

"I'm offerin' ya a night ya'll never forget, where I fuck ya like you ain't never been fucked before." Redneck Joe said, looking like he was ready to spit on the floor, or maybe his face always looked like that.

"As amazing as a night on the air mattress in your trailer sounds," Ashley said, being as sincerely perky as he could manage, "I think I should warn you that my boyfriend just got released from prison today and should be meeting me here any minute. And, well, ever since he caught me sleeping with his best friend, he goes crazy if another guy even looks at me. That's why he was doing time." This was Ashley's favorite lie to get rid of a guy, and it was always fun watching their reaction as they processed the story. It always worked too. Their expression would either turn terrified as they skittishly looked around for said boyfriend, or they would stare at him like he was crazy, in which case, he would play along and swat his arms at imaginary dragons flying in front of his face while muttering something like, "No! Dragon dog, you can't have my shoe, I need it to walk!" Redneck Joe appeared like he was still ready to spit, but he walked away not even saying a word. *How rude*, Ashley thought.

Maybe now he could relax and enjoy his drink. Less than a minute later, another guy walked up and stood by his table. Ashley hoped that by blatantly ignoring him, the guy would go away. No such luck, however. He slowly turned his head, ready to tell the guy to "beat it," but no words formed in his mouth when he saw the large bulge of an obviously hard cock. He slowly forced his gaze up to meet the prettiest blue eyes he'd ever seen. He thought the guy might have said something by the way his lips moved, but if he did, Ashley didn't hear anything.

Ashley knew he'd have to flirt and talk to a few guys to prove he could pass as a woman, but he hadn't thought a man this attractive would approach him. And that bulge, *fucksticks,* it made his mouth water. He wanted to taste it and have it burst in his mouth. Clearing his throat, tall, dark and studly asked, "So can I buy you a drink?"

Smiling as sweet as possible, Ashley purred, "You don't need to buy me a drink, honey. I'll suck your big cock right now. Bathroom or alley?" Ashley wouldn't even try to deny that as soon as a big cock came his way, he went from Ashley to Trashley, but damn, that was slutty even for him. He didn't have any time to waste tonight though. As soon as he saw that huge bulge, he knew he had to have it. And he'd have to get it quick, before he slipped or somehow exposed himself as a man. Ashley knew he would have this man's cock in him soon, one way or the other, even if he had to slide under the table and blow him right here. That thought sounded really hot actually; and if he was going to act like a slut, he might as well go for the full gusto.

"As hot as that sounds, I think I'd rather buy you a drink first. I'm Rick," he said with the same confident smirk that was making Ashley uncomfortably hard. His cock was securely tucked up between his thighs by his tight, red panties. Luckily, he was sitting with his legs open under the table so it had a little more room to expand. Rick's smirk clearly said,

"I'm Rick, and yes, that is my big dick you're staring at, and yes, I'm going to make you wait before you can get a closer look." Ashley could play that game too, only he hoped to speed things up a little. He'd have to really lay on the charm and make sure Rick saw the small, silver barbell sticking through his tongue. When a guy sees someone they find attractive with a pierced tongue, they can't help but imagine it stimulating their cock, something Ashley planned to use to his full advantage.

"I'm Ashley," he said in his most sensual voice. "I like long walks on the beach, eighties music, and anal sex. I'm the kind of *girl* who will do *anything* sexually." Sticking his tongue out, Ashley slowly rubbed his piercing along his bottom lip, "You also might be interested to know that I have no gag reflex." Ashley smiled when Rick quietly moaned while adjusting his huge bulge before he sat down across from Ashley. "I'd love to get on my knees and worship every inch of your thick cock."

Ashley watched Rick squirm a little in his seat, once again having to adjust his cock through his tight jeans. "You're very direct. I like that. You're also very beautiful, and I think I'd like to sit here and get to know you more." Damn Rick, Ashley couldn't afford to sit here and get to know him better. The longer Rick sat there looking at him and talking, the more likely he would notice Ashley was a man.

If Ashley was dressed as a guy and Rick had shown interest, he would have loved to get acquainted before moving on to getting physical. Rick was tall, handsome, charming, with a wicked smile and what looked to be a killer package. Too bad he was also straight and thought Ashley was a woman. Otherwise he would totally date or fuck him repeatedly, whichever Rick wanted. Instead, he apparently had to up his game, blow him as soon as possible, and leave before Rick realized who he stuck his dick in. Ashley would probably feel bad about being so deceptive in the morning, but right now, he just needed Rick's big cock.

****

Rick felt Ashley's foot start to rub the back of his leg under the table before Ashley opened his naughty mouth. "I'd love to get to know you better, Rick. Love to hear how loud you get when I take you deep in my throat and swallow around your cock." Ashley wet his lips again, flaunting the piercing Rick was lusting to feel. "What about you, Rick? What do you want?" Ashley asked with a silky purr. He was a master at seduction.

Rick wasn't sure how to answer that question. Well, honestly, he wanted to bend Ashley over the table and fuck him right here, but he worried that if he said as much, Ashley would have them in that position within seconds. He really didn't want to get kicked out of the pub; he liked it here. Rick was about to answer with something generic like asking to know where Ashley worked or something similar when he felt Ashley's foot start to creep up his thigh.

Rick quickly moved his hands down to stop the foot before it reached his cock. He would probably blow in his jeans if Ashley started rubbing against his erection, as he was already aching for release. Looking down, Rick moaned when he saw Ashley's foot just a sliver from reaching its target. Ashley still had his heel on, his toes sticking out of the open end. Rick wanted to suck on those cute toes and see how Ashley responded to that.

Keeping Ashley's foot in place, Rick started rubbing the smooth skin around Ashley's ankle, moving slowly up his leg. When he looked up, Ashley just grinned before raising his eyebrow questioningly. Rick knew he was asking, "Ready for that blow-job now?" And, God, was Rick ever ready, but he didn't want to say that until he was sure Ashley wouldn't disappear after. He wanted this to be the first of many fucks, potentially the start of a kinky relationship if they hit it off more than just physically, and he had a sinking feeling Ashley was in a hurry to blow n' go.

"I want another beer. What are you drinking, sweetheart?" Rick made sure to phrase his question in what he hoped was straightforward enough to avoid any sexual innuendos.

Ashley grinned. "This was a rum and coke." He pointed to his still half-full glass. "I'd much rather drink your load, though." He finished by winking at Rick and using his teeth to play with his piercing. *Fuck*, of course Ashley would make the simplest comment sexual and hot as hell. And damn, the thought of releasing down Ashley's throat was enough to make him *almost* forget he was trying to make sure this went beyond one sexual encounter.

Reluctantly pushing Ashley's foot out of his lap, Rick stood up, "I'll be right back with those drinks" before heading to the bar. He made sure to lean against the bar so he could keep an eye on Ashley. He had a feeling that some of the bluntness of Ashley's statements actually came down to nervousness. Rick wanted to make sure he didn't try to leave while he was getting their drinks.

When Rick got back to the table a few minutes later, Ashley was still just sitting there playing with his tongue piercing. Rick set the rum and coke in front of Ashley while sitting back down. "I've always found words so meaningless. Everyone is always talking so much that what they say just has no substance. I'm not going to say, 'Thanks for the drink, Rick.' Instead, I'd rather show my appreciation by sucking your dick. What do you say, Rick? How about letting me show you my gratitude now?"

Everything Ashley said made it harder for him to not just give in and let them both get what they wanted, but he was still not convinced Ashley wouldn't just disappear when they were finished. Rick decided he would keep trying to start a conversation even if it was looking impossible to get Ashley to discuss anything but sex. "What's your favorite color?"

Ashley groaned before answering, "Red, it's fierce and passionate. I love watching my skin flush red after a long, hard fuck." Oh hell, Rick tried to make conversation, but this was just too much. The picture Ashley just described had him too turned on to think. Rick needed to clear his head and get his thoughts together. Making excuses about needing to piss, he stood up and headed to the toilets. Maybe if his erection died down he could get some blood back to his brain. Then he could start an actual conversation and get to know Ashley a little more. But it was hard to stick to that plan when he was near Ashley when all he could think about were those killer legs, tight ass, and wicked mouth.

****

Ashley waited for Rick to close the door before following after him. He noticed earlier the bar had three unisex bathrooms, which would be a little more private. Ashley hoped Rick forgot to lock the door behind him so he could slip in, drop to his knees and show Rick just how stupid talking was when he could have Ashley's lips stretched around his cock instead.

Saying a small "thank you" when the door opened, Ashley slipped in as quietly as possible, locking the door behind him. Rick was standing at the one toilet with his back to the door. He obviously didn't hear the door open, or if he did, he knew it was Ashley and didn't bother to turn around. Ashley set his little red purse on the small counter next to the sink.

He walked up behind Rick, placing his hands on his hips. "I'm too hard to piss," Rick said quietly. Ashley pushed with his hands, turning Rick around so they were facing each other. Rick didn't say anything else, but he also didn't act surprised, so he must have known Ashley would follow him. "I can take care of that for you," Ashley responded just as quietly as he slowly crouched down on his heels. He really didn't want his knees touching the floor, since that was just gross. Rick had his jeans unzipped, his cock sticking out through the opening. It was already so hard that the foreskin had retracted. It definitely looked hot, with just his cock sticking out, but Ashley also wanted to play with Rick's balls.

Unbuttoning Rick's jeans, Ashley grinned when he discovered Rick wasn't wearing any underwear. He slowly pulled the jeans down Rick's thighs. Tired of waiting, Ashley raised his eyes to Rick's, making sure Rick was watching as he leaned forward and took Rick's entire length down his throat. "Fuck!" Rick roared in surprise before moaning loudly. With his face pressed against Rick's crotch, Ashley took a deep breath through his nose. Rick smelled manly but with a hint of peaches. Ashley briefly wondered what kind of body wash Rick used before getting back to the blowjob.

He brought one hand up to cup Rick's large balls hanging low under his cock. With his other hand, he moved around to squeeze Rick's muscular ass. He bobbed his head a few times, enjoying how much Rick stretched his mouth as he moved back and forth. Ashley stopped massaging Rick's balls to bring his hand up and wrap around the base of Rick's cock. It was time to show Rick just how much fun a tongue piercing could be.

****

Rick braced his hands against the walls of the small room to help remain steady on his feet. He never had anyone suck his cock so well or swallow the full length so easily. Then Ashley used his hand to pull Rick's foreskin back up around the head of his cock. Ashley slid his tongue in between the foreskin and the head of his cock, the piercing adding extra stimulation Rick had never felt before. His knees almost buckled, and he started thrusting his hips, more by reflex than any conscious thought. Ashley started moving his tongue around the head as he used his hand to stroke up and down Rick's shaft, adjusting to Rick's thrusting rhythm. Rick was moaning louder and more continuously as

Ashley pushed the foreskin back up against his tongue before pulling it down again.

Then Ashley pressed the end of the piercing into Rick's cock slit. The sensation was overwhelming and Rick wasn't sure how he held off coming. Ashley's tongue felt un-fucking- believable, too good.

"Stop!" Rick ordered. He couldn't take any more without coming. "I want to fuck you."

Ashley pulled off Rick's cock with a *pop*. He nodded to Rick before putting his hands on his knees and pushing himself up. He walked a step over to the sink, grabbing something out of his purse.

Holding up a condom, Ashley said with a wink, "Aunt Flo's visiting and she's got the front door locked down tighter than Fort Knox, I'll let you sneak in the back though. It's a lubed condom and I already did some prep work, so you can just suit up and slide home." He finished by bending over, putting one hand on the counter while the other pulled his panties just below the swell of his perfect ass. He pulled his skirt up completely exposing his bare backside.

He obviously thought Rick hadn't already figured out he was a man and was doing everything he could to make sure Rick didn't find out. Rick didn't know if that was part of the thrill for Ashley, thinking he was seducing straight guys or if he was just worried how Rick would react if he found out. Rick didn't care either way, but there was no way he was going to fuck him in that position. He had other plans.

****

Hearing Rick open the condom, Ashley turned to watch over his shoulder as Rick rolled it down his cock. Turning his head back around when Rick started walking up behind him. He was surprised when Rick grabbed his hips and spun him around before setting him on the edge of the counter. He had no time to react before his legs where being lifted up making him lean over until his back hit the wall. Rick had Ashley's legs in the air and was pulling his panties off over his heels before Ashley even knew what was happening. Rick dropped the panties on Ashley's purse. Ashley was thankful the counter was built onto supportive cabinets making it sturdy.

"Hold your legs up," he ordered and Ashley immediately grabbed his legs behind the knees holding them in place, slightly panicking because when Rick looked down he would see Ashley's hard cock and exposed balls now that they were no longer trapped by the panties. "And relax, I know you have a dick," Rick said as he pulled his shirt over his head, tossing it by the panties. His chest was hairy, although not overly thick and it was trimmed. He had enough hair to run your fingers through but still see his dark nipples and a stunning tattoo. It was a large, dragon sketched in vibrant black lines. The dragon's head was over his right pec, the mouth was open, and its tongue was colored with a striking red, while the eyes were a soft shade of gold. The rest of the dragon wasn't filled in with ink. The body trailed down his torso and the tail wrapping around his lower abdomen and curling around his naval, with the tip flaring out to point down towards Rick's dick. He had a slight beer belly, but it was small enough that if he sucked it in, it would be almost flat.

Ashley wanted to lick every inch of that tattoo, following the trail back down to Rick's juicy cock. He was so mesmerized by Rick that it took him a minute to realize what Rick had said. "Wait, how did you know I was a man, and why didn't you say something sooner? I used all my best techniques to get you off quickly, scared you'd notice I was a guy and kick my ass. And yes, I know I would have deserved it for trying to trick you, but you're so hot and when you walked up to my table with that huge cock bulging in my face, I just had to have it," Ashley smiled weakly at Rick. "And being, uh, prepared is just sort of habit. I had no intentions of actually sleeping with anyone tonight."

"I knew the minute you walked in that you were a man," Rick said moving his hand to Ashley's neck and rubbing his thumb over Ashley's Adams apple. "You should have worn a chocker or something to cover your throat. If it helps at all, the straight guys were too busy looking at your rack or ass to notice. And I didn't say anything because I didn't know if you thought of yourself as a woman or just dressed as one. It didn't matter to me either way; you're beautiful, and I wanted you the moment you stumbled in while yelling insults at people trying to leave."

"Oh," Ashley muttered. "I rarely do drag and mostly just do it to wear the shoes. I definitely like being a man," Ashley said as he watched Rick lean in closer. "And that guy started it."

"The shoes are hot. I'd like to see you in just the shoes. I'd like to fuck you in just the shoes," Rick whispered before he leaned in and kissed Ashley. It was a sweet, tender kiss that Rick ended before it got heavy. "Let go of your legs and put your feet on my shoulders."

Doing as Rick instructed, Ashley felt Rick positioning the head of his cock against his hole. Rick put both of his hands on Ashley's thighs as he pushed his cock into Ashley's ass. Ashley groaned as Rick continued pushing until his cock was completely sheathed inside him. After giving Ashley a minute to adjust to his dick, Rick began a steady thrusting rhythm. Ashley watched as Rick turned his head and slowly ran his tongue up the side of his black high heel.

When Rick reached the opening on the end, he sucked Ashley's big toe into his mouth. Ashley bit his bottom lip and tried to muffle his whimpering. *Holy Mother of Fucking*, he had never seen anything as hot as Rick licking his stiletto while pounding his thick cock into Ashley's willing hole.

Pulling his lips off Ashley's toes, Rick turned and said, "Your heels are so hot. I could suck on your toes all night." Rick grunted and started thrusting more. "And the way your ass grips my cock-"

"Jesus, Rick, just shut up and fuck me. Dirty talk is for foreplay not while fucking. You have an awesome dick, now shut up and use it."

"You in a hurry, Princess?" Rick grunted as he started thrusting harder and faster. "Jus' wanna hurry up and get off?" Rick muttered.

Ashley shook his head. "Quite the opposite, in fact. If you keep talking like that, my cock is going to blow too soon."

"Ah, don't want to hear about how I'm going to take you home tonight, strip you naked, except for the heels, and fuck you senseless, then, do you?" Ashley shook his head as he bit his lip harder, willing his body not to come before Rick was ready. "Or how, in the morning, I'll take you on my glass dining table?" Rick teased.

"Fuck, Rick, I can't wait anymore," Ashley panted as Rick wrapped his hand around his cock, only pumping a couple times before Ashley was coming all over Rick's chest and stomach. Ashley really appreciated that Rick made sure Ashley's jizz landed on his own bare chest instead of Ashley's top or skirt. And Rick looked damn fine with Ashley's spunk dribbling down his hairy chest.

Rick kept pumping a few more times before he stilled with his cock buried deep in Ashley's ass. When he finished coming, he gently pulled out and tossed the spent condom in the toilet. Rick then lowered Ashley's legs to the ground and helped him sit back up on the counter.

"I got you all dirty, Rick, better let me clean you up," Ashley purred before leaning forward and slowly licking his own come off Rick's belly, starting at the tip of the dragon's tail he worked his way up to Rick's chest. Once he was satisfied he'd licked every inch clean, he looked up at Rick who let out a low growl before wrapping his hand around the back of Ashley's neck and bringing him in for a rough kiss. Rick pushed his tongue into Ashley's mouth, taking complete possession of it; all Ashley could do was whimper and hang onto Rick's strong shoulders.

"Get your panties back on, Ashley, if that is, in fact, your real name. I have more plans for you tonight," Rick said as he slipped his own shirt into place.

He smiled at Rick, "Wouldn't you like to know my real name?" Ashley couldn't help winking at Rick and teasing him before seriously responding, "Ashley is my real name, it'd be too much work trying to remember a different drag name, I'm lucky my name works for both genders. Now, about these other plans you have, I can't wait to see what else you have in mind."

Rick gave a mischievous smirk and his eyes lit up with uninhibited desire, promising that the night was only going to get hotter. That had Ashley rushing to get his outfit decent enough to walk out of the bathroom without drawing too much attention. "Let's go." Ashley said as he took Rick's outstretched hand. Rick quickly led him through the bar, as they were both eager to get on with the rest of the evening. As they were making their exit, Ashley thought to himself that, unless he counted that douche Redneck Joe, not passing as a woman was one challenge he didn't mind failing.

Dirty Drag 2

The Night Continues

Ashley still couldn't believe that barely an hour ago he'd hooked up with a stranger in the bathroom at a dive bar. Well, Rick wasn't just any stranger; he was a hot, sexy, make-your-insides-melt stranger. After the raunchy restroom sex, Ashley accepted an invitation to finish the night back at Rick's place. That's how he found himself sitting in Rick's kitchen while Rick prepared them something to eat. They needed to keep their energy reserve stocked, and if Ashley had his way, they would need it. Still, he wasn't sure if spending more sexy time with Rick was smart, or if he was an idiot to be going home with a man he just met who could turn out to be some kind of psycho killer, especially since Ashley hadn't told anyone where he was going. If he washed up dead, no one would remember seeing a guy leave with Rick, since as far as anyone could tell, he'd left with a woman.

However, as Ashley watched Rick's back flex while he cooked, he decided that he was ninety-six percent sure Rick wasn't a killer. Four-percent was a minimal risk, and Ashley's gut told him Rick was a genuinely nice person. Ashley couldn't help his thoughts though, and they were scattered all over the place. One second he wondered why they weren't naked yet, the next he was back to serial killers. Ashley didn't know why he was so jittery, probably something to do with being in an unfamiliar situation. They'd already fucked and now Rick was inviting him over for the night and cooking for him. It seemed intimate, and Ashley wasn't sure how to feel about that.

He knew that just sitting there and watching Rick wasn't helping; he needed a distraction. They hadn't really talked since leaving the bar, other than Rick asking him if he liked French toast. Ashley, of course, had replied that it made him salivate just thinking about swallowing a big, warm mouthful of that delicious goodness. Saying something slutty was his default response when he was nervous or unsure of himself, especially around someone he found attractive. And he found Rick more than attractive. He was fucking delicious, but Ashley still couldn't hold back his abrasive retorts.

"I don't cook." Ashley decided it was best to get some stuff out in the open. He wasn't sure where Rick wanted this encounter to go, but in case they did somehow develop a relationship, he wanted everything on the table from the beginning. It avoided arguing and miscommunication down the road, assuming this lasted longer than a night. "I mean, I can cook, but I choose not to, it's too much of a hassle. Everything worth eating can be nuked in the microwave, and it tastes just as good."

Rick skeptically looked over his shoulder at Ashley, "No, it doesn't."

Ashley shrugged, "You get used to it then."

"That's okay I'd rather not get used to it, besides, I *can* cook. Maybe you can ..."

"I don't clean either," Ashley cut Rick off before he could offer the 'I'll cook, you clean' compromise. Attempting to be a little more accommodating, Ashley added, "I'll load the dishwasher, but I don't scrub anything."

"I was going to say maybe you can make up for not cooking with *other* skills, but if you don't clean either..." Rick shrugged and just left that statement hanging, insinuating that Ashley's "other skills" wouldn't make up for his phobia of common household chores. *As if!*

"My body can bend like a pretzel, and I can do things with my mouth that make porn-stars envious. And stamina? Yeah, I got enough of that to outlast the Energizer Bunny." Ashley said proudly, with a hint of defensiveness.

Rick turned around and slowly looked Ashley up and down with intense scrutiny. Ashley fought against his instinct to shift away and avoid Rick's inspection. Ashley knew he looked like a hot mess. For one, his legs were open and clearly visible under the glass dining table. His skirt was short enough that Rick would be able to see his panties, and he'd given up all pretenses of tucking after their earlier adventures. He could feel Ashley junior and the dangling orb twins trying to escape the lacy fabric. The padding from his left breast was out of alignment, and rather than fixing it, he just crossed his arms, causing it to pop out completely. Ashley pretended not to notice as his cheap imitation boob landed on the floor. However, what probably looked the worst was that he'd taken off his wig and hung it on Rick's coat rack. His own short, brown hair didn't compliment the makeup he was still wearing, even when it hadn't been smothered under a wig for hours. Ashley didn't even want to imagine how many sweat clumps his hair had formed or how raggedy he must look.

Ashley refused to appear self-conscious, so he wore an expression that he hoped looked smugly confident when Rick finally met his gaze. "I think you'll have to prove that before I can believe you." Rick said casually. Oddly, he seemed unaffected by Ashley only having one boob, as he turned back to the stove. Ashley noticed the playful challenge in Rick's words though. Ashley liked challenges, and he had a compulsive need to beat them. Even more than a challenge, he liked how Rick seemed to be at complete ease with him. In drag, in half-drag, it never felt like Rick judged him.

Ashley didn't want to analyze how he felt about Rick's acceptance though. If this were just a one-night stand for Rick, Ashley would rather not build expectations if that were the case. He decided to focus more on proving his sexual proficiencies. That would be easier if he didn't look like the bride of Frankenstein's even uglier stepsister. Ashley politely excused himself before heading to the bathroom Rick had shown him during the tour Rick gave him when they'd first arrived. He quickly started looking for something to remove his makeup and made a mental note to start carrying his facial cleanser and makeup remover pads with him.

The best thing Ashley could find were some moist towelettes sitting on the counter. He thought Rick must take his personal hygiene seriously, a habit they had in common. Ashley grabbed a couple wipes and started rubbing the makeup off his chest and then his face, hoping they wouldn't be too harsh for his sensitive skin. Next, he washed his hair in the sink with warm water and towel dried it. Ashley studied himself in the mirror His skin was a little flushed from the wipes, but it wouldn't last. His hair was artfully messy, just the way he liked it.

Without the wig, makeup and missing boob, he looked ridiculous in his low cut top. That was a simply fixed problem. He took his top and bra off. Oh yeah, that was way less ridiculous, wearing just his miniskirt and stilettos. The perfect attire for breakfast at Tiffany's Whore House. Hopefully, being nearly naked would probably get things to quickly transition into activities of a more adult nature. Ashley licked his lips and smiled at all the possibilities the rest of the night held.

With one last glance in the mirror, he strode back to the kitchen. Rick sat at the end of the table with two plates set and ready. Ashley took his seat beside Rick, keeping his back straight and his head held high. Ashley heard of some people not knowing what to say on dates and there being long pauses of awkward silence, but Ashley had never experienced that problem.

"What the hell is this, I thought you said you were making French toast?" Ashley questioned, looking at the unidentifiable mound on his plate.

"There's French toast on there. I just made it dirty French toast by piling crushed Oreos on top and then adding a drizzle of maple syrup." Rick said, nodding his head at Ashley's plate. "Just try it."

"I um, have never had French toast this way before. It looks ... interesting" Ashley said. He didn't want to lie and say it looked delicious, but he also didn't want to be rude and say it looked disgusting. Moreover, he didn't want to seem boring and say he preferred old-fashioned French toast, but he wasn't sure he was adventurous enough to try this diabetic's nightmare on a breakfast-plate. "You must be a fancy gourmet chef or something." Ashley tried to say flirtingly, as he picked up his fork and started pushing his lump of crushed Oreos around. What Rick referred to as a drizzle of syrup, Ashley called a flood. The Oreos had absorbed a lot of the syrup, making a soggy, unidentifiable looking mixture. The excess syrup was pooling around the edges of the plate.

"Shut up and try it." Rick said sharply, "And if you want more Oreos, they're in there." Rick nodded towards his Death Star cookie jar in the center of the table. It was probably the most awesome thing Ashley had ever seen, but he kept that to himself. He didn't want to nerd-out when he was trying to be coolly confident.

"I think I have plenty of Oreos for now. I always thought Oreos were the most superior cookie. I mean, you can do so much with them, like lick them, twist them apart, dunk them in a glass of milk, or crumble them and use them to bury French toast. How are the other cookies supposed to compete with that?"

Rick just gave him a look that clearly said 'shut up and eat.' Ashley wasn't sure if he should be intimidated or impressed with Rick's ability to communicate so easily without words.

"I want to try it, I really can't wait to taste this heavenly looking, um food. It just seems so divine I can't decide where to start." Ashley said, doing his best to make his words sound like they were sweeter than honey.

"Start by putting it in your mouth." Rick stated dryly. Ashley decided he needed to work on his sweet voice.

"I'd like to put something else in my mouth," Ashley gave Rick a sly grin, running his tongue piercing across his bottom lip. Ashley remembered the real reason he was there, and he was a little surprised the strange food almost made him forget. "I think I might be more in the mood for sausage."

"I thought that lame line was reserved for pizza delivery guys." Rick said before taking a big bite of what looked like dirt piled on his fork.

"I don't know who delivers your pizzas, but I have yet to see a delivery guy worth using a line on. And if I did, I'd probably use 'nice shoes, lets fuck,' since they're on a schedule and don't have time for subtle flirting."

"I don't think you have any idea how to be subtle." Rick retorted with a teasing smile.

"You've known me for like an hour. You lack the necessary time required to make an assumption like that." Ashley stated factually, but unable to hide his own smile. He didn't think Rick believed him.

Rick simply raised his eyebrow, clearly asking 'who're you trying to fool?' Ashley figured it was best to just eat and get it over with. It couldn't taste that bad. Then, he could get Rick fully naked and have some fun, assuming he didn't get sick from breakfast. Ashley scooped up a small bite and quickly ate it. He'd never seen pig slop before, but he imagined it was probably about the same texture as this. Nevertheless, it didn't taste too bad, just very sweet and a bit odd. It was something he couldn't really describe, and if asked, he would just tell people to try it themselves.

The loud, sensual moan he released as he slowly pulled his fork from his closed lips was just for Rick. "No one makes sounds like that when they eat," Rick said unfazed by Ashley's attempt to sound sexually enticing.

"It was the thought of having my mouth stuffed full of something else that had me moaning." He winked at Rick. Then he scooped up another bite and moaned even louder as he gradually pulled the fork from between his lips. His next bite he made sure had extra syrup that he *accidentally* let drip on his chest, "Oopsie, it looks like I made a mess." Ashley used his finger to scoop up some of the syrup. Making eye contact with Rick, he smoothly sucked his finger into his mouth. He knew he had Rick's attention when he heard him groan. "You going to help me clean up or just watch me struggle to get all this syrupy goodness wiped up by myself?" Ashley asked in a low, husky voice.

"You're mostly just smearing it around and making it worse. I'd better help before you start getting it on the furniture." Rick said, grabbing Ashley's wrist so he could pull the syrup-coated fingers to his lips. Rick closed his eyes as he sucked two fingers into his mouth. Ashley let out a small whimper and quickly used his free hand to drip syrup around both of his nipples and down the center of his stomach.

Rick released his fingers and opened his eyes. He smiled when he looked at Ashley. "Already made a bigger mess I see." He stood up and pulled Ashley's chair out far enough that he could kneel between Ashley's spread legs. He leaned over and pressed his lips against Ashley's, careful to make sure their upper bodies didn't touch. The kiss deepened as their tongues collided, pushing against each other.

That lasted until Rick started trailing kisses along Ashley's jaw, down his neck, and finally reaching his chest. He started by sucking and licking on Ashley's right nipple. Ashley was lost in the moment and wasn't sure if he was mumbling encouragement or just moaning, but he knew he was the one making soft noises. After finishing with the right nipple, Rick moved to the left one, giving it the same tantalizing treatment. Then he slowly started licking the line of syrup running down the center of Ashley's chest. While his mouth was busy on Ashley's stomach, Rick used his hands to unzip Ashley's skirt. He tapped Ashley's hips letting him know to lift up. Rick leaned back enough for Ashley to close his legs and let Rick remove his skirt and panties.

Rick let his searing gaze slowly travel over Ashley's entire body. Ashley resisted the urge to blush. He would let Rick look as long as he wanted to. Rick's eyes stopped at Ashley's feet. "You look so fucking hot with only your heels on." Rick said, licking his lips. Ashley followed his tongue's movement and couldn't resist moaning at the sight. With a sigh, Rick continued, "It's too bad I need to take them off." He took his time slowly removing Ashley's heels, using the opportunity to rub Ashley's feet. With the heels removed, Ashley was left sitting there completely naked while Rick was still entirely dressed.

Before Ashley could tell Rick to get naked too, his cock was sucked deep into Rick's warm, wet mouth. It was an unexpected sensation and Ashley instinctually bucked his hips up and let out a hoarse groan. He watched as Rick bobbed his head up and down, working his cock only using his skilled mouth. Ashley could see Rick's arms were moving, he assumed Rick was unbuttoning his own jeans. Ashley could hear the lowering of Rick's zipper. The movement of Rick's shoulder helped Ashley imagine Rick slowly stroking his own cock from the base to the tip. All the while, his mouth never faltered in the rhythm he'd set sliding up and down Ashley's hard dick.

Rick braced his hands on Ashley's knees. He pushed them further apart and forced Ashley to slide closer to the edge of his seat. Rick pulled Ashley's cock out of his mouth and ordered, "Keep your knees spread apart." Then he started sucking on just the head of Ashley's cock, his tongue licking and teasing the underside. Rick's hands started slowly moving down Ashley's legs. When Rick reached Ashley's ankles, he clamped his hands around them.

He lifted them up and started to bring them together. Ashley felt his knees start to close, until a glare from Rick reminded him to leave them open. Rick brought the soles of Ashley's feet together so they were touching and positioned just above Rick's lap. Rick fully swallowed Ashley's cock at the same time he thrust his own through the arches of Ashley's feet. He must have already spread his pre-come around his cock because his thrust glided smoothly between Ashley's feet. Ashley knew he had a high arch so it probably wasn't as tight a grip as Rick would have liked. As Rick slowly thrust between Ashley's feet, Ashley could tell he was really enjoying it.

Rick increased the speed at which his mouth was masterfully working Ashley's cock. It didn't take long before Ashley was warning Rick, "I'm going to shoot."

Rick didn't slow down or pull away. When Ashley released, it was with his cock lodged deep in Rick's mouth. Rick carefully put Ashley's feet back on the floor. He waited until he was sure Ashley was finished coming before pulling his mouth off Ashley's cock. "Delicious," Rick licked his lips while looking up. "You still need a shower though. You're all sticky."

"You didn't come yet." Ashley protested.

"I'm saving it for later." Rick grinned smugly at Ashley. "For now, you go start the shower, and I'll clean this up real quick," Rick motioned towards the dishes on the table. "And then I'll join you." He patted Ashley's thigh before he started picking up the dishes.

Ashley just nodded and used the table to help push himself up, he wasn't sure how steady his legs would be after his intense orgasm. After he was sure he was stable and his legs wouldn't give out he slowly made his way to the bathroom. He ignored the fact that the bottoms of his feet were sticky and hoped he wasn't leaving a trail for Rick to clean up. He wanted to argue and demand Rick let him bring him to climax right now, but he refrained. It didn't seem fair that he'd just had a mind-blowing climax and Rick was stuck cleaning up without any release. Ashley figured that Rick might get off on being in charge so he'd do what Rick said. For now. He would guarantee that, before the end of the night he would make Rick blast at least one more load.

Ashley let the water heat up before he stepped into the tub. He wasn't sure if he should take his time, letting Rick have a chance to join him. He decided to go about his normal bathing routine. If Rick did join him in the shower, that'd be great. If not, well, he would be fresh and clean for some debauchery between the sheets.

Ashley finished washing and turned the water off, he wasn't sure how long he had been in there but he had not heard anything from Rick. Pulling the shower curtain open, he stepped out of the tub and grabbed the towel he'd used earlier. With his back to the door, he started drying off his feet and then worked his way up. He had made it all the way to his hair when he felt hands grab his waist and a large naked body press up against his back. Ashley was surprised but didn't flinch, he hadn't heard Rick enter the room and admired his ability to be so quite. Ashley dropped the towel and pushed back into Rick.

"You have the sexiest ass." Rick's voice was husky, his warm breath against Ashley's ear sent a delightful shiver down Ashley's spine.

"It's yours." Ashley whispered as he shoved his ass more firmly against Rick. "You can have it *any way* you want..."

Rick groaned deeply and readjusted his position behind Ashley. His hard cock slid into the crevice between Ashley's ass cheeks. He slowly thrust his cock up and down, Ashley moaned every time it rubbed over his opening. Rick nipped his earlobe before grunting, "Any way I want?"

Ashley's mouth had gone dry and he had to swallow before he could respond, "If you want it, take it."

Rick responded to Ashley's remark like the challenge it was. Rick tightened the grip he had on Ashley's hips and spun him around to face the counter. "You might want to hold on." Rick ordered. Ashley didn't see anything to grab so he braced his hands against the counter top.

He felt Rick's hand on his lower back, forcing him to bend slightly over the counter, and causing his ass to stick out more. It also allowed Rick's cock to make longer strokes in Ashley's cleft.

"Your ass drives me crazy." Rick sighed. He used his hands to squeeze Ashley's ass before he pushed the firm mounds together. Forcing them to mold around his cock and giving him a tighter, more enclosed cavity for his cock to plunge into. Ashley could see Rick's reflection in the mirror. Rick grinned smugly as he looked down to where their bodies met.

"Like what you see?" Ashley moaned as Rick started rubbing harder over his still sensitive hole, sending a jolt through his body every time. Even without any stimulation on his dick, he thought he might come again just from the sensations.

Rick looked up and met Ashley's gaze in the mirror. Ashley noted that there was a pleased glint in his eyes. "You have no idea how much I want you." Rick grunted. "Feeling your ass caress my cock, and watching myself slide between your lush cheeks, it's enough to make me come." Rick moaned.

"Do it," Ashley whimpered, "Come all over me. Cover me with it." Ashley felt Rick thrust a few more times before he watched Rick close his eyes. Rick's mouth fell open as he let out a deep groan. Ashley felt his come land on his back, it sparked his own smaller release. He'd never gotten off like that before, something about the way Rick took control and worked them both into complete satisfaction caused Ashley incredible pleasure he'd never experienced before. Ashley didn't know how many shots Rick released before he finished climaxing. They both stayed like that, waiting to catch their breath and get their pulsing bodies back under control.

Rick stepped away for a few seconds and Ashley felt the damp towel he used earlier wipe the semen off his back. When he was done, Rick tossed the towel aside and pulled Ashley up and around so they were facing each other. Rick leaned down and gave him a deep kiss. When he pulled back he quietly asked, "Ready for bed?"

Ashley licked his lips and just nodded.

Unglamorous Day Drag

"What time is it?" Ashley groggily asked, stretching his arms over his head. He smiled remembering the night before with Rick. Even though after they left the bathroom they only went to bed and made-out for a bit before snuggling together and drifting to sleep, Ashley felt content. He could hear Rick moving around in the bathroom. It felt like he'd just gone to sleep when Rick was waking him up, but he surprisingly didn't feel that tired. Didn't mean he was ready to get out of bed yet, though.

"It's early." Rick sounded a lot more awake then Ashley.

"Why are we up then?"

"I have to be at my parents' house by eight thirty. We're doing a weekend camping trip, and I promised I'd be there. I already have my stuff loaded in my truck or I'd have had to get up even earlier."

It was too early for Ashley to even think about camping. Did he even know anyone that had ever been camping before now? He certainly hadn't been. "That sounds like a really fun time," being stuck in the woods surrounded by family. Ashley didn't say the last part aloud.

"Yeah, we like to do something as a family at least once a month. It'll be a good time." Rick stepped into the bedroom, he was already dressed and freshly shaven. He smiled at Ashley apologetically, "I'm sorry I have to rush you out of here."

"Oh," was all Ashley said, as he suddenly realized he wasn't sure how to get home. He couldn't walk home in the outfit he was wearing last night. He'd probably be mistaken for a hooker and end up being arrested. In addition, he really didn't want to have to sit in a taxi like that either.

"That's cool, Rick. I should probably get home anyway. Is there any possibility that you might have a shirt I can borrow or something?"

Rick seemed to think about it for a minute. "You know I think my sister left something here that will fit you. I'll be right back." When Rick returned, he was carrying a gray hoodie and also Ashley's skirt, panties, and heels. "I put your other stuff in a bag by the door."

"When you said 'rush,' you weren't kidding." Ashley mumbled. He was naked as he got out of the bed and walked over to Rick, "I'll take these and use the bathroom and be ready in a jiffy."

Before Ashley could turn towards the bathroom, Rick stopped him by cupping his cheek. "I really am sorry we have to be in such a hurry." He rubbed his thumb along Ashley's bottom lip. "I'm just not sure how long it will take to drive you home, and I don't want to keep the family waiting." He leaned down and gave Ashley a quick kiss. He thought it was really sweet of Rick to anticipate his need for a ride home and to then take the time to drive him.

When Rick pulled out of the kiss, Ashley smiled appreciatively up at him and said, "A ride home does make up for rushing me around."

Ten minutes later, they were at Rick's front door and Ashley had just finished straightening out his messy wig. He pulled his large sunglasses out of his bag and slipped them on. "So, how do I look?"

"Beautiful." Rick responded.

Ashley just laughed and reached out to give Rick a playful shove, "I know I look like a mess. I'm wearing my slutty skirt and stilettos, my wig is in complete disarray, and I'm not wearing a speck of makeup." Ashley looked down at his chest. "But what really completes the ensemble is that I'm wearing a sweatshirt that barely stretches below my belly button and says 'I Love my Little Pony' with a picture of two ponies and a rainbow."

"Hey, that sweatshirt is adorable." Rick said, sounding like he was trying not to laugh as a big smile formed on his lips.

Ashley shook his head and looked in the plastic bag Rick had left by the door. It had his bra, boobs, and the top he'd worn the previous night. He dropped his purse in there as well so he'd only have one thing to carry. "I think this will still draw less attention than my slutty top would, and I appreciate you letting me borrow it." Ashley said sincerely. "I'm ready when you are."

The Ride Home

"So, are you going to offer me your number?" Rick asked, after Ashley gave him directions to his apartment.

"Why, so you can call me for a booty call?" Ashley responded enthusiastically.

"No, so we can go on a date, hang out and get to know each other better."

"Maybe you misunderstood me. I want the booty call! Plus, we already did that, remember? When we met, you said you wanted to get to know each other, so we talked for like twenty-five whole minutes before hooking up in the bathroom."

"We need more than just sex. I want us to get to know each other and build a relationship that will last even if the sex becomes routine."

"Well," Ashley said to buy himself some time. Rick had seen most of his personality quirks and seen him looking tragic in various states of half drag. And he still wanted a date. Ashley knew he should probably jump on this chance. After all, Rick seemed like a great guy and he *was* hot. Still, he felt the need to make sure Rick really saw what he was like. He didn't want to waste time dating if they were going to break up over some little thing down the road. "I guess we can go out sometime and just see where things go. You do already know I don't cook or clean. I'm also very competitive, and I like to get my way."

"You snore," Rick added.

"I do not snore!" Ashley said outraged. "Take that back!"

"Don't worry, it was a cute snore. It was really soft and reminded me of when I was a kid. Our golden retriever would curl up and cover his nose with his tail, and every now and then, he'd let out a little snort." Rick said smiling.

"You didn't just say I snore like a dog."

"I said it was cute." Rick justified, "You're the one who started listing your faults; I was just contributing to the list. And you should know, the more excuses you make for why we won't work, the more determined I get to prove you wrong."

"I didn't really need help with that list, thanks." Ashley said, nudging Rick's shoulder with his own. "I guess since I've charmed you so much, the least I can do is let you take me out sometime."

Rick dropped Ashley off with a passionate kiss and a promise to get in touch when he got back into town on Sunday.

Welcome Home Surprise

When Ashley stepped out of the elevator on his floor, he could see a man knocking on his door. Even from the back, he could tell by the tight jeans and designer shirt that it was his kind-of-a-friend, Jared. Okay, he's really Ashley's best friend, but Ashley still thought about jumping back into the elevator cab, if only the doors hadn't already closed. With a sigh, Ashley walked up and tapped on Jared's shoulder.

Spinning around, Jared said with false sincerity, "I'm sorry," and without missing a beat added, "Ms. Lohan. Did I disturb you?" Nodding at Ashley's door he continued, "My friend won't wake up and he turned his phone off."

Ignoring the gibe about looking like Lindsay Lohan, Ashley asked, "Did you ever consider your friend might not want to see you this

- 144 -

early?" Ashley fumbled around in the plastic bag for his phone. Finding it, he said, "Phone's dead." He waved it in the air for Jared to see.

"Holy fuck!" Jared sounded shocked. "Ashley, what the hell happened to you?"

Ashley glanced down at himself. Yeah, he was a mess, but he couldn't be that bad. "Nothing happened to me."

Jared studied Ashley a little closer before asking, "Then why do you look like a sickly crack whore?"

"Day drag." Ashley answered simply. "The sun turns vampires to dust and drag queens into this." He motioned with his hand down his body. "Now, will you move so I can unlock my door?" Ashley would like to avoid running into anyone else in his current state.

"Please do," Jared gestured to the door while stepping out of the way. "I'm having an emergency and need to borrow a Q-tip, pronto."

"You came all the way over here for a Q-tip?" Ashley finished unlocking his door, and they stepped into the apartment.

"I met a guy last night. He lives in this building but he did not have a single Q-tip!" he crossed his arms and sighed heavily. "I think his name was Bruce."

"And you couldn't wait until you got home for one?" Ashley questioned skeptically.

"No, I could not wait." Jared said resolutely, heading towards the bathroom. Ashley went to his room and placed his wig on his vanity, he would brush it out later. He tossed the plastic bag on his bed. Changing into a pair of sweats and a t-shirt, Ashley walked back into his living room.

Jared seemed disappointed standing in the middle of the room, both hands in his jean pockets. "It didn't work. I can still feel it in there," he said, giving Ashley a pleading look.

"I have no idea what you're talking about." Ashley said, feeling confused.

"It's Bruce's fault!" Jared said animatedly. "The bastard didn't warn me he was a long distance shooter. He hit me right in the ear with one of his spunk cannon fires. Luckily, I had my eyes closed." Jared flopped down on my couch. "How could he not warn me first? That's rude, right?" Jared looked at Ashley, who nodded in consent. "He should have handed me a pair of earplugs and said 'You'll want these, it's going to be a wet ride!' At the least he could have mentioned something about the front row being in the splash zone."

"That's more information than I would ever need." Ashley stated, sitting down beside Jared.

Jared ignored him and continued, "Then Bruce is all like 'Let me clean that up for you,' or I think that's what he said. I only had one working ear at that point. And before I knew what was happening, he was leaning down and thrusting his tongue in my ear." Jared shook his head a little, "like that would help. All he did was push his jizz further into my ear and make it even nastier with the extra saliva." Jared closed his eyes and made an expression as if he was reliving the memory. "After the shock wore off, I begged for a Q-tip." Jared opened his eyes and looked directly into Ashley's eyes, "I fucking begged, Ashley! He didn't even have a cotton ball! That's why I'm here. But, it is too late now. All the man juice has dried up, and it feels crusty. It's making my ear itch." Jared explained, again sharing excessive information.

"Are you done? Because I don't think I can stomach anymore of your details."

"Yeah, I think that's it," Jared said softly, "I mean, we were having a really great time, it was smoking hot. Then, without warning, he erupted like a gushing geyser. Total mood killer." Jared looked at Ashley, "I'm glad you look normal again. Druggy streetwalker is just not a look you can pull off sweetie." Ashley glared at him. "Stop looking at me like that and start telling me what has you doing the ultimate walk of shame this morning."

Ashley filled Jared in about what happened the previous night, leaving out the specifics and adult content. As over the top as he might be, he still didn't like to talk about intimate and sexual details, even with friends. When he finished with his story Jared responded, "Oh honey, you know I was drunk and just teasing you. Until I saw you this morning, I thought you always looked gorgeous." He smiled at Ashley.

"Shut up." Ashley nudged their shoulders together. "I didn't look that bad this morning. And you're doing the walk of shame right now." Ashley gestured towards Jared's outfit, obviously the same one he wore last night.

"But, I still look cute, no shame in that. You looked like a dirty mess." Jared stopped and appeared to be thinking, "Although I did honestly think you were an authentic party girl. So you can pass as a biological-train-wreck-of-a-woman and even fool your friends." Jared said, clapping his hands as if he had just given Ashley great news.

"You have a gift for words and always know what to say to make a person feel good." Ashley said sarcastically.

"That's true." Jared smiled, "Take me home now. I need to look up how to get dried baby batter out of my ear canal."

"Call a cab. And for the love of God, never talk about come in front of me ever again." Ashley begged.

"I promise I'll never talk about a man's sweet cream in front of you again, if you give me a ride home." Jared offered.

"Deal!" Ashley immediately responded before Jared could try to change the agreement. Having already been out looking worse, Ashley just slipped on his flip-flops and took Jared over to his place.

Blackmailed into a Happy Ever After

It was early Sunday evening when Ashley got a text message from Rick. *I have your boob. If you ever want to see it again, you'll have to meet me for dinner tonight.*

Ashley didn't even need to think about a reply. *How do I know you really have my boob and this isn't a trap?*

A few minutes later, Ashley received a picture of his left breast padding. He hadn't even noticed it was missing from his bag. In the picture, the boob was leaning against Rick's wicked cookie jar, with a tiny plastic Storm Trooper holding a gun, pointed right at the padding. There was also a note in black, block letters: 'DINNER, OR THE BOOB GETS IT!'

Ashley couldn't help but grin as he replied, *Fine. I'll be there. Where will the exchange go down?*

Dairy Queen at 6:30pm. Come alone.

With the rendezvous set, Ashley knew he needed the perfect outfit for this exchange. He smiled, his thoughts spinning, as a plan formed to turn the tables on his blackmailer.

Dirty Drag 3

Getting Serious

Ashley had a plan; he was going to dress as the sluttiest skank ever, even if he was meeting Rick at the local Dairy Queen and not some club. It would serve him right for the atrocious kidnapping of his left boob. Rick deserved the surprise. Then after thinking about it for a few minutes, Ashley chuckled lightly realizing that probably wouldn't actually shock Rick at all. In fact, he would most likely be expecting it. After all, in the short time they had known each other — um, more like in the one night they had spent together, all he did was act like a rampant sex fiend.

Ashley knew he didn't really want to be thought of like that, not by Rick anyway. He would be a fool to let Rick slip away, and he had no doubt that's exactly what would happen if he didn't start acting like an adult capable of having a relationship. That is what he wanted right? A chance to see how they connected with each other, more than just physically. Rick had already put up with a lot, more than he probably should have, and yet, he still asked Ashley out. Ashley wasn't stupid. He knew Rick could only bend so far before he just gave up on Ashley.

So, he decided to take this date seriously. He'd use this opportunity to impress Rick and show him that he did, in fact, have more to offer than just being a sexy skanktart. To show that he wasn't *just* a brainless bimfoon, that's when a bimbo breeds with a buffoon, resulting in a true, hot mess. Ashley smiled to himself as he walked over to the far side of his room, just past his vanity and opened his closet, pushing clothes out of his way. He knew just what he wanted to wear, and it was hiding in the very back of the full closet.

Drag Queens spend a lot of time looking in mirrors, at least Ashley did anyway. Not just while applying makeup but he also spent a lot of time making faces in the mirror. He knew he looked ridiculous, but he had to see how his make-up appeared when he made certain expressions. Blending and shading was an art, and he had a style all his own. Some poses made his cheeks look bloated or pressed his eyebrows too close together, resulting in the dreaded unibrow. That had happened once when he was first getting used to applying make-up. In fact, he found drawing eyebrows especially hard, so he always scrutinized himself, scrunching up his nose and squinting his eyes. Any unflattering expression he made sure not to use out in public. After he has finished painting on his makeup and he's thoroughly inspected his work, he always blows himself a kiss in the mirror.

Tonight, there would be no need for drag makeup, but that didn't mean he wouldn't still wear some. Sitting down at his vanity with large swivel mirror, he applied light charcoal eyeliner, just to help outline his big brown eyes. Then he put on some clear but shimmery lip-gloss, making his lips look soft and inviting. He smiled at himself in the mirror, thinking Rick wouldn't know what hit him when he showed up looking serious and professional. Ashley blew himself a kiss in the mirror. He may not be in drag, but he still looked delicious, if he did say so himself. Getting up, Ashley grabbed his jacket and headed out the door. He had one fake-titty to collect and a man to impress.

A Date at the DQ

Ashley didn't see Rick when he got to the prearranged rendezvous point, also known as Dairy Queen. He walked in and got a booth towards the back along the wall. It wasn't even close to private, but it was the best he could get. He would have ordered their meals but, with the extensive menu selections, he had no clue what Rick would want. He sat down and patiently waited. Okay, he waited, but he wasn't very patient about it. He tried crossing his legs, but the table was too low so when that didn't work, he tapped his foot on the floor.

He felt almost as nervous as he had on the night he'd met Rick, only then it had been the fear of Rick's reaction to finding out he was impersonating a female. As it turned out, Rick knew all along and liked Ashley in both the slutty women's clothes or as a man. He even seemed to like him in a messy in-between state of dress.

This was different though. Instead of trying to hide who he was, he was going to show Rick the real him. He couldn't help but worry that he was making a huge mistake. What if Rick didn't like what he saw? Or worse, what if ordinary Ashley wasn't spunky enough and he bored Rick? It was a risk, but one he knew was worth taking. That, however, didn't stop him from still worrying about possible negative outcomes.

By the time Rick arrived, Ashley still hadn't gotten his anxieties under control. Nevertheless, when Rick approached the table grinning with one sexy dimple showing, Ashley felt himself relax. Even if Rick turned out not to want to pursue a relationship, Rick would never use anything Ashley revealed against him. Nor would he lead Ashley on and then be cruel. Rick was far too nice for that.

"You look ravishing," Rick drawled in a deep voice. "Maybe a little over dressed for the DQ though." He smiled, and Ashley could feel the heat from Rick's eyes devouring him, taking in every detail. If Ashley hadn't already sensed Rick's desire from his heated stare, the growing bulge in Rick's jeans would have clued him in.

"This old thing?" Ashley teased, even though Rick's reaction was exactly what he hoped for. That's exactly why he had worn this suit, a deep purple button down shirt, a vibrant red silk tie, and black jacket. He'd slicked his hair over from the left to the right. Ashley thought he looked damn good and it seemed Rick agreed. Rick himself was looking mighty scrumptious, wearing well-fitted blue jeans and a tight black t-shirt with the phrase "Trust Me, I'm a Jedi" printed in white letters across his chest. It was a simple outfit, but he made it look good, and, of course, the way he filled out the front of his jeans was wicked sexy. The only way Rick could possibly look any more appealing was if he was naked.

Noticing Rick still hadn't sat down, Ashley asked, "Did you want to eat, or did you want to go somewhere else?" After he finished speaking he immediately shut his lips and started pushing his tongue ring against the back of his teeth. It was a nervous habit, but it allowed him time to wait for Rick's response without his mouth filling up the silence by adding a lewd suggestion for why they should leave.

"Let's go order." Rick said, gesturing for Ashley to go in front of him. As Ashley passed by, Rick placed his hand on Ashley's lower back and walked beside him towards the counter. Standing next to Rick without his heels on made him feel much shorter. He wasn't self-conscious about it, but it was definitely registering in his mind as he stood side by side with Rick in only his flat dress shoes.

The kid working the register appeared to be about sixteen and gave them a funny look, though it was probably more because they were dressed like complete opposites rather than because of how close they were standing. After casually checking to make sure Rick wasn't paying attention, Ashley opened his eyes wide and stuck his tongue out at the gaping cashier.

His friend Jared often told him that his ears popped out when he did that, causing him to look like a monkey. Having practiced the face in the mirror several times, Ashley had to agree with him. The kid actually laughed, and by the time Rick stopped studying the menu and looked at him, Ashley's only expression was a sweet, innocent smile. Rick raised his eyebrow, silently asking, '*What did you just do?*' Ashley just shrugged and kept on smiling.

After carefully considering all of the gourmet dinner choices, Rick ordered the savory Mushroom Swiss burger with a medium Oreo Blizzard. Ashley got the moist and tender chicken strip basket, which came with marvelous gravy and a soda. Ashley quickly paid, since he was the one with a boob to save. As they stood waiting for their food, their sides pressing together, Ashley basked in Rick's embrace enjoying the comfort and intimacy. He was delighted with the knowledge that Rick liked touching him, because he definitely liked to be touched by Rick. Rick's hand never lost contact with Ashley's back. He was continuously rubbing small circles or just letting it rest on his lower back, until Rick needed his hands to carry the tray of flavorful smelling food back to their table.

They were back in the booth, sitting with the food on the table in front of them when Rick asked, "So, what did you do to that kid?"

Ashley feigned a reaction of appalled shock and was about to ask why Rick would insinuate such things but he came up with a better question. "How bad do you want to know?" Rick raised a questioning eyebrow that Ashley took to mean, *'I'm not answering that.'* Ashley shrugged and continued on, "Well," he folded his hands on the table in front of him, "it seems we each have something the other wants." He used his most sinistery villain's voice, which sounded more like he had a sore throat than anything else. "Tell me what you've done with Lucy, and I'll give you the information you seek." Ashley grabbed a fry, dipped it in his rich gravy, and then took an exaggerated bite in an attempt to show his fierceness.

Rick just watched him, patiently. Ashley could tell he was trying hard not to burst out laughing, probably so he wouldn't draw more attention than they were already getting. "Who is Lucy?" He asked, before wrapping his lips around a spoonful of his Blizzard, a little bit of ice cream dribbled down from the corner of his mouth.

Ashley had a hard time focusing as he watched Rick wipe away the drips with his tongue, but he finally managed to say, "Lucy is my left boob, which you're currently holding hostage. That is why you brought me here, isn't it? To commence negotiations?"

- 153 -

"You named your breast pads? Why Lucy?" Rick said, taking a bite of his burger.

Ashley finished chewing the fry he was enjoying before answering. "Lefty Lucy," he said, drawing it out so it sounded more like loose-y and following it up with, "Duh."

Rick shook his head, laughing quietly before asking, "Do I want to know what you named the right one?"

Ashley pretended to consider that for a minute, "Probably not."

Rick leaned forward, "Tell me anyway."

"Righty Tighty, because it is perky and tight, and not much else rhymes with righty that makes any sense." Ashley thought about what he'd said, "Or as much sense as a man naming his fake breasts can make."

"You're a nut." Rick said teasingly, taking another big bite of his juicy burger.

Ashley ripped one of his succulent chicken fingers in half and thought about what Rick said. "I think if I was a nut, I'd be a chest nut." After a few seconds, he quickly added, "No pun intended."

"Because they have a prickly shell you have to break before you can peel back the skin to even get to the edible part?"

"No, because they taste fu--" Ashley paused and looked around at the other guests, "absolutely delicious."

Rick had been displaying a dazzling smile when his expression went blank. "So are you ever not in drag?" He wasn't condescending or judgmental, or meaning to be cruel. He asked it out of sincere curiosity.

The question still felt like an accusation and was a shock to Ashley. He didn't think he could have been more surprised if, out-of-the-blue, Rick reached across the table and bitch slapped him. No longer hungry, yet feeling the need to defend himself, Ashley dropped his fry back in the box and placed his shaking hands in his lap so Rick wouldn't see them. When they said goodbye Saturday morning, Ashley had pointed out a few of his own flaws, wanting to prevent awkward dating if he wasn't what Rick was looking for in a boyfriend.

Now, he was sitting here wondering what he did wrong and knowing Rick was looking at him and expecting a response. Ashley bit his lower lip and tried to buy himself a little time by looking thoughtful. Hopefully, Rick would think he was pondering the question and taking it seriously, which he was. Nevertheless, he also wanted to get up and just leave, telling Rick he was sorry for wasting his time. But Ashley wasn't the type of person to run away from a situation just because it would be the easier thing to do. He still didn't know what to say, so he replied with a simple and meek, "I'm not in drag now."

"I mean, I doubt you're a suit and tie at the Dairy Queen kind of guy. So you're really wearing another kind of costume." Rick stated without a hint of disdain in his words.

Ashley gaped at him before lowering his head to stare at the table. So much for trying to show Rick he was taking getting to know each other seriously. He felt like he'd fucked it up royally and didn't even know how. Or was it because he dressed too serious for Rick to take him seriously, which *seriously* made no sense to him. This is who he is, and he thought Rick was seeing that. Finding out how wrong he had been made his chest feel restricted, and he had to remind himself to keep breathing.

He liked Rick, a lot, and wanted to be honest with him. Rick made him feel safe opening up about himself, and if he didn't do a better job of putting himself out there and letting Rick see the real him, he knew he might not get another chance. He just hoped he hadn't already blown this one. "You said you wanted to get to know each other, and I want that too. I wanted to show you I was taking this seriously and wanted to impress you. That's why I dressed seriously impressive." Ashley met Rick's eyes, "That doesn't mean this isn't the real me. Yeah, I wear a lot of outfits, but underneath, they're all a part of me. They all make up who I am."

Rick just smiled at him; it was a warm, inviting smile. "I think that's the most sincere thing you've ever told me. I saw you so dressed up and just assumed you were being another character. For that, I'm sorry." He sounded genuine, and Ashley let out a small sigh of relief, pleased he hadn't blown his chance with Rick. Well, not yet anyway.

He opened his mouth to say something sarcastic, to lighten the mood, but decided against it. "It's okay, with how I've acted, it's no wonder you'd draw that conclusion. But I mean it. I'd like to get to know you." Ashley swallowed, "For us to know each other."

Rick's smile broadened. "I'd like that."

"So, how do we do that?" Ashley asked.

"With time." Rick stated simply.

"You're a man of few words." Ashley smiled slyly.

"And you're a man of many." Rick said with a teasing glint in his eyes.

"Touché. But really, I'm not very good at this, and I already feel like I know you."

"Yeah?" Rick spoke softly, "what do you think you know?"

"I know you're thoughtful. When you had to meet your family, you still took the time to drive me home. And you're loyal and keep your word, like how you passed up a day of sex with me to go camping, keeping your prior commitments. You're a considerate lover, making sure we both get the most pleasure possible. You cook and clean and wouldn't mind if I didn't. If I'm being honest, you could probably find a way to bribe me into cleaning up." Ashley gave him a wink. "Your place is neat and welcoming, which says a lot about you. I know you have a good sense of humor and smile a lot. You have a foot fetish, and it doesn't bother you that I have one for heels and doing drag. You have a sweet tooth and like Star Wars. I know you like dogs, or at least had one growing up. And that

- 156 -

you like cuddling and having me close, even in public. I know you're really patient," Ashley smiled, "with me at least."

"I think -" Rick started, but Ashley interrupted him.

"I'm not finished yet. I could probably spend another hour coming up with little things I've already noticed about you. We could sit here and talk about your favorite color or your childhood best friend, but that's not how I get to know people. I know that it's not as easy to get to know me like that, and that's my fault for putting up fronts. And, you know what? I like all that stuff about you, and I want you to learn stuff like that about me." Ashley paused and took a deep breath before adding in a softer voice, "And hopefully you'll like what you learn."

"I was trying to say I think we should leave and finish talking later."

"You haven't finished eating yet." Ashley pointed out. He hadn't either, but he didn't plan to finish his meal since his mind and appetite was fully on Rick.

"I'm not hungry, not for that anyway." Rick nodded at his food before letting Ashley see the burning desire in his eyes. More than just seeing the craving in Rick's expression, it was as if Ashley could feel it. His body responded, and he could feel his cock starting to get hard in his slacks. He was really glad that he wasn't tucked, but still, there wasn't much room for growth in his panties.

"Oh," Ashley said, catching on to why Rick wanted to leave. "Hearing how great you are gets you going, does it?" Ashley teased him a little.

"It wasn't hearing how great I am; it was the way you said it and knowing that's how you see me that has me wanting to take you right here on the floor of the Dairy Queen."

"Rick, you almost sound like me." Ashley said playfully.

"You must have rubbed off on me."

"If I remember correctly, it was you who rubbed off on me." Ashley reached down to adjust his now full erection.

"Seriously, are you going to invite me back to your place, or do I have to drag you out to my truck," he lowered his voice so Ashley had to lean forward to hear, "and fuck you across the bench seat?"

"I thought you wanted us to get to know each other better." Ashley clarified wanting to make sure this wasn't a trick to see how serious he was.

"Is a night spent having passionate, animalistic sex going to make it harder to get to know each other?"

"It's making something harder." Ashley mumbled. "So you want to come back to my place for some raunchy sex?" He said more cheerfully knowing Rick wanted to go to his place because it was closer.

In lieu of answering, Rick just stood up and motioned for Ashley to do the same. When Ashley wasn't quick enough, Rick grabbed his arm and helped him to his feet. With a hand on his lower back, Rick led him towards the exit. "Wait," Ashley protested, "we have to bus our table."

Rick growled, but started quickly loading up the tray with their garbage. After dumping it in the trash bin, they walked outside with Ashley leading the way, Rick following right behind him. "I'll walk you to your car." Rick whispered against Ashley's ear. The warm breath against his skin made Ashley's spine tingle, and he felt himself relaxing back against Rick's chest. Rick's hand found its way to Ashley's hip and pulled their bodies tighter together. Ashley let out a low moan feeling Rick's arousal pressing against the top of his ass. "I want you, but I don't think they'd appreciate us fucking in front of their entrance. Where's your car?" Rick asked, stepping forward and forcing Ashley to move with him.

Taking the hint, Ashley picked up his pace and hurried over to his car. "This one's mine" Ashley said, stepping next to his Silver Prius. Rick looked through his front window and started laughing. "It was a gift from a friend." Ashley said, explaining the amusing air freshener hanging from his rearview mirror. It said 'I'm only speeding cuz I have to poop' on it in rainbow colored letters.

"It suits you." Rick said stepping up to him so his back was against the car door, plastering his front against Rick. Reaching out his hand, Rick grabbed the back of Ashley's hair, tilting his head up, and crushing their lips together. It was rough, demanding, and told Ashley just how ravenous Rick's desire for him was burning. Ashley moaned into the kiss, and Rick used the opportunity to thrust his tongue into Ashley's mouth. His hands were just starting to feel up Rick's chest when Rick broke the kiss and stepped back. "I'll meet you at your place." Rick said before walking a few spaces over to his truck. Ashley stood there for a few minutes catching his breath and trying to get his body cooled down enough to drive home. He felt like his brain melted from the heat of that kiss.

Ashley Gets Pregnant!
Just Kidding. They Do Have Sex Though

Rick was waiting outside the front entrance of the building by the time Ashley had parked his car in the lot. He figured Rick must not have needed as much time to cool off as he did before being able to drive. Ashley used his access card to open the doors and led Rick down the entry hallway, and past the mailboxes to get to the elevators. Rick didn't try to touch him this time, and Ashley figured that was for the best if they wanted to make it all the way to his apartment.

Stepping into the elevator, Rick said, "You still never told me what you did to the kid working at DQ."

It took Ashley a couple seconds to remember what he was talking about, "And you never gave me my boob back."

"Here." Reaching in his back pocket, fumbling for a few seconds, he pulled Ashley's precious Lucy free and held it out to him.

Ashley took it from him and noticed there seemed to be a few more lumps than when he last felt it. "Now it's all lumpy, you goober. They aren't really meant to be stuffed into a back pocket or sat upon."

"Really?" Rick asked, grabbing the boob from Ashley and examining it. "Sorry, I didn't think it would get deformed like that." Rick said sheepishly, "I'll buy you a new one."

"Don't worry about it. They're cheap, and I have extras anyway."

"So," Rick said, not meeting Ashley's eyes, "now that you technically got your boob back, are you going to tell me now?"

"Fine," Ashley sighed heavily for dramatic effect. "If you must know, I made a monkey face at him."

The elevator doors opened, and Ashley stepped out. He didn't make it very far before Rick's hand on his arm stopped him. Turning so they were facing each other, Rick said, "Show me, please." Ashley hesitated, but decided there was no reason not to show Rick. Besides, the man did say please, and he was simply too cute to say no to. Ashley reenacted the monkey face, and Rick instantly started laughing. Ashley let his expression relax back to normal. "Oh man, your ears." Rick said between laughs. "They look so cute sticking out like that." Ashley tried to glare at him, but Rick ruined it by caressing his cheek and then gently rubbing his earlobe between his thumb and forefinger. His other fingers curved around Ashley's neck slipping under his shirt collar. "Seriously," Rick said huskily, "everything about you turns me on."

"I can see that." Ashley nodded towards the bulge in Rick's jeans. "And luckily, I've had twenty five years to get used to these ears, so I'm not overly sensitive about them." Ashley tried to distract himself from just how much Rick's warm touch was making his knees feel weak.

Rick pulled him into another scorching kiss that only lasted mere seconds, but Ashley felt it from his lips to his toes. "Nothing to be sensitive about. You're one hundred percent perfection just the way you are." Rick told him sincerely. For the first time that Ashley could remember, he felt himself start to blush, even as his stomach did summersaults. That was also the first time he'd ever heard anything so sweet, and he knew Rick meant it, making it all the more sweeter.

"I think we should go inside." When Rick made no move, Ashley took a step backwards and Rick stepped with him. When Rick took another step, Ashley stumbled backwards, but Rick moved his hand to his lower back and steadied him. "This would be easier if you let me turn around."

Rick shook his head slightly, "I like looking at you. Which door is yours?"

"Number nine zero nine. It's the fourth door on the left." Ashley wasn't sure how far they had already walked down the hall, and he didn't want to look away from Rick. Occasionally, Rick's eyes would dart over to check their progress down the hall, but mostly his gaze remained locked on Ashley.

After only a few awkward stumbles, they stopped and Rick said, "Keys?" Ashley pulled his key chain out of his front pocket and held up the one for his unit. Rick took it and after unlocking the door, forced Ashley back into his apartment. Ashley felt a shift when Rick moved his leg back slamming the door. "I think we should head right to the bedroom. Okay with you?" Rick asked sounding breathy, the desire in his voice adding to Ashley's own deepening needs.

"That," Ashley swallowed, "sounds divine." Ashley had no trouble navigating his way backwards into his room through his small apartment. They were still holding eye contact when they reached the bedroom, stopping next to the bed. In the privacy of Ashley's bedroom, the feeling of intimacy increased substantially, leaving Ashley suddenly unsure how to proceed. Luckily for him, Rick didn't have the same issue. Sliding his hand slowly from the back of Ashley's neck until it reached the knot of his tie, Rick gave a gentle tug. Ashley gasped when the back of Rick's warm knuckles grazed his throat, the exquisite sensation sending another slow shiver rippling through his body.

Ashley reached up and wrapped his tingling fingers around Rick's forearm. He wasn't sure why, but something about the connection made him feel anchored, steady. He didn't have to worry about his knees giving out, because he knew Rick wouldn't let him fall. He watched a sensual smile slowly creep up Rick's lips as he gently loosened Ashley's tie. He didn't remove it though, or even completely untie it but just loosened it enough that he could start unbuttoning Ashley's shirt.

Not a word was spoken, but Ashley could feel the tension between them charging up, getting ready to explode. With his shirt undone, Rick popped the collar up and pulled the shirt out from under the tie loop. Forcing Ashley to release his hold on his arm, Rick slid both the shirt and the jacket off Ashley's shoulders. Ashley closed his eyes and just enjoyed the feeling of Rick's feathering touch against his skin. When his clothing hit the floor, Ashley remained standing there in just his slacks and dress tie. Ashley opened his eyes and a shiver tingled down his spine, again. It wasn't because he was cold, it was because of the way Rick licked his bottom lip while looking at Ashley as if he was the most desirable man in the world. Like the *only* man in the world.

Dropping to his knees, Rick started untying Ashley's shoestrings. "This will be easier." Ashley said, pulling his foot back so he could toe off his dress shoes, which he quickly kicked out of the way.

"Easier is not always better." Rick offered, as he started removing Ashley's socks.

"Easier is better if it means we get naked faster." Ashley contradicted with a broad smile.

"Patience is a virtue." Rick slipped off the first sock, taking his time to gently massage Ashley's foot.

"Why put off to until tomorrow what you can ravage right now?" Ashley countered, keeping up the banter with Rick was all that was distracting him enough to keep from prematurely blowing his load in his panties. His cock hadn't even been touched yet, but Rick had him close to plummeting over the edge of excitement into a blissful orgasm.

"Good things come to those who wait." Rick said, grinning up at him, his expression of satisfaction making it clear he knew how much he was affecting Ashley.

"Why wait, when you can procreate?" Ashley said, trying not to giggle as Rick's light touch on the bottom of his foot slightly tickled.

"We can't procreate, not together any way." Rick said casually.

"You asshat." Ashley said teasingly. "That's a minor technicality, but fine. Why wait when you can fuckreate?"

"Because waiting makes it that much sweeter or because some things are worth the wait. Pick one." Rick said, in the same playful tone Ashley had just used. He finished pulling Ashley's socks off and slid his hands inside the legs of his slacks along his calves, rubbing Ashley's legs.

"Really? Because this wait feels like it wants to kill me." Ashley hoped Rick would hear the plea in his voice and speed things up. He wasn't sure how much longer he could hold off before he'd have to take matters into his own hand. He preferred for it be Rick's hand or mouth that brought him the release he needed.

Leaning forward, Rick nuzzled his cheek against Ashley's groin. Ashley's body initially jolted from the unexpected contact before he consciously pushed his hips forward, enjoying the soothing pressure against his hard cock. "You feel fine to me." As Rick spoke, his lips moved against the shaft of Ashley's dick.

"Did you know that it can take sloth's days to have sex?" Ashley stated. Rick pulled back and gave him a concerned look. Ashley ignored it and continued. "With the pace you're setting, I'm thinking you could be part sloth."

Rick's jaw dropped, and he just gaped at him before a big smile spread across his face. "I don't know why hearing that surprises me. Only you would come up with something like that during foreplay." Then he reached out and placed his hand over Ashley's erection with the barest of touching. "I was ready for fast and rough when we left the DQ, but on the drive over, I started thinking about how I haven't taken my time with you yet. And I love this slow and unhurried, sloth pace." Rick growled, leaning forward he scraped his teeth lightly against the fabric restraining Ashley's erection. "Maybe if you didn't talk so much it would go quicker." Rick said, giving him an affectionate smile so he'd know he was still teasing.

"Talking's the only thing keeping me distracted enough to not come in my pants." Ashley bit his bottom lip, hoping it would help him prevent doing just that. Ashley sighed with relief when Rick's fingers started fumbling with the button on his slacks. *Now we're getting somewhere* he thought, *finally*.

"Oh hotcakes. That's fucking sexy." Rick groaned after lowering Ashley's zipper and getting a glimpse of his panties showing through. "I was going to keep teasing you, but fuck it, now I've got to see just what you're wearing underneath these slacks." He said, shoving the pants down and then off Ashley's legs. "Sexiest thing I have ever seen."

Ashley smiled at Rick's eager reaction. Besides the tie still loosely wrapped around his neck, he was standing there in just his skimpy, red, lace panties with a slutty black frilled trim. The panties were tight enough and the fabric thin enough to clearly see Ashley's raging erection. Ashley thought of it as raging because it felt like it had been achingly hard ever since he saw Rick's sexy body walk into the Dairy Queen. "You haven't seen the back yet." Ashley pointed out, twisting his hips so Rick could just see the bubble of his ass.

"You going to turn all the way around and let me get a good look?" Rick's gaze was locked on the panties.

"Only because I don't believe in torturing people by slowly teasing them to death, and I   like having your attention."

"Huh? You're still talking, why aren't you turning around?" Rick let his eyes drift up to meet Ashley's so he could see the humor in them and know Rick was only kidding.

With Rick in front of him, and the bed behind him, he didn't have much room to do anything but simply turn around. He tried to make sure his hips swayed suggestively, but there just wasn't space to do it properly. He was planning to keep spinning all the way around, but Rick's hands on his ass stopped him. "Let me just look for a minute." Rick growled. Ashley wouldn't complain, as he liked Rick's hands massaging and squeezing his globed cheeks. Ashley felt Rick leaning in closer, his warm breath gently teasing against the left side of his ass.

"Hey!" Ashley yelled and forcefully spun around after Rick's teeth nipped his butt. "That was mean." He rubbed his cheek, but the sting was already dissipating. Mostly his reaction was just surprise, but it still seemed rude to bite someone's butt without consent, even with gentle playfulness.

"I couldn't help myself, it was just too tempting." Rick licked his lips. "You are the epitome of every fantasy I've ever had, all rolled into one devilish, sexy package." Rick said breathlessly staring up at him. Retaining eye contact, Rick leaned forward and put his mouth over Ashley's panty-covered cock. He suckled on the head before opening his mouth wider so his lips would also rub against Ashley's shaft. He used his tongue to lick the underside of his cock head the through the thin lacy fabric.

"Oh, oh God!" Ashley moaned loudly. Between Rick's sweet words and the amazing lip job on his cock, Ashley felt himself losing control under the dual assault. He moaned as the pleasure from his orgasm rolled through his body. His knees started to buckle, but Rick's firm grip on his hips helped to keep him steady. Rick closed his mouth as tight as he could around the head of Ashley's cock. Sucking the jizz spurting from

Ashley's dick through the fabric until Ashley had to push him away because he was getting too sensitive.

"Delicious." Rick said sticking his tongue out so Ashley could see his come that Rick hadn't yet swallowed. Rick raised an eyebrow at him and Ashley took that as asking, 'want a taste?' He felt like he should be embarrassed for coming so quickly, but obviously Rick didn't mind and he was too content to worry about it.

"Come up here with that." He said, after taking a moment to catch his breath. His voice still sounded rough because of his dry throat, but Rick was about to take care of that. Standing up, Rick wasted no time crushing their lips together, pushing his tongue into Ashley's waiting mouth. He moaned into the kiss tasting himself on Rick's tongue. The kiss deepened as they swapped spit and Ashley's release back and forth. Ashley found himself with his tongue thrusting into Rick's mouth. He could still taste himself mixed with Rick's own natural flavor. Rick was using his teeth to gently bite and manipulate Ashley's piercing.

Ashley wasn't sure how long they had been kissing when Rick pulled back and rested their foreheads together. They stayed like that smiling at each other, feeling the other's warm breath dance across their lips as they steadied their breathing. Ashley was the first to break the silence. "It's like I can think again now that the edge has been taken off."

"And what are you thinking about?"

"How, once again, I'm basically naked, fresh off a spectacular orgasmic release and you're still fully clothed and needing to come." Ashley said, shaking his head in slow, exaggerated movement. "That just won't do." He grabbed the hem of Rick's shirt and pulled it up, exposing Rick's torso. Ashley used the opportunity to rub the back of his fingers against Rick's skin. Lending a hand, Rick grabbed the shirt from Ashley and removed it completely in one quick motion. "Hey, I was going to do that." Ashley protested weakly, as he touched his fingers to the dragon tattoo on Rick's chest. As far as he was concerned, the faster Rick got naked the better, but after Rick's torturous teasing he felt he should protest for the spirit of protesting. That didn't really make sense, but Ashley didn't care. It wasn't as if Rick could read his thoughts.

"That was easier." Rick mimicked Ashley's earlier comment. "Besides, you don't seem to mind too much." He finished, sounding a little smug.

Ashley was transfixed watching his hands tracing the dragon's body winding down Rick's stomach. He still managed a small reply, "I do like it easy." His fingers reached the arrow point on the end of the Dragon's tail just under his belly button. Rick's breathing was shallow and steady, but as Ashley's hand kept drifting lower, he sucked in a deep breath. Ashley didn't waste any time unsnapping the button on Rick's jeans. Remembering that Rick liked to go commando, he slipped his hand into the opening of Rick's pants and covered Rick's bare cock before lowering the zipper. He pushed the jeans off Rick's hips and all the way down to pool at his feet. "I love that you're not wearing underwear." Ashley wrapped his fingers around Rick's fully erect cock and let it spring up to a more comfortable position before slowly stroking it. Ashley enjoyed the moaning vibrations that emitted from Rick's throat because of his touch.

"Not sure you should do that unless you want me coming in your hand." Rick growled.

"Guess now would be a good time to make things easier by kicking off your shoes and jeans." Ashley said, fixated on watching Rick's cock head disappear and reappear behind his foreskin as Ashley moved his hand back and forth. "And I can think of much better places for you to come than in my fist." Ashley looked up at Rick's face and whispered, "Like inside my ass."

"Okay, I'll get my pants off if you stop touching my cock before it explodes." Rick said starting to work his shoes off, a task made more difficult by the jeans around his ankles. "After all, if you want something done right, you just have to do it yourself." He said, in a strained voice, going back to their odd flirtational adage exchange.

"A horny man always knows when to ask for help reaching faster gratification." Ashley joked, as he stepped back from Rick to give him more room, freeing his legs.

"Where do you think you're going?" Rick reached out grabbing Ashley's tie. He gripped the silky fabric and pulled Ashley back to where he had been standing. "You look so hot wearing just your panties and tie." Rick finished kicking away his jeans and shoes. "Only thing sexier would be if you had a pair of heels on."

"I," Ashley cleared his throat, "could always put on a pair of stilettos."

"This time, I want us completely naked. Next time you're going to wear your favorite heels and these panties. And I'll fuck you in just those."

Ashley's only verbal response was a deep moan. He felt his heart speed up. Rick's promise made his body feel like it was on fire with a new, deeper desire. The way Rick took control, and knowing they shared at least some of the same fantasies, made him blaze with the need to experience all of them with Rick. Taking a deep breath, he tried to reign in his excitement before he came again without Rick having even one orgasm.

"Finish stripping and get on the bed. I need to be inside you again." Rick ordered, pulling the tie over Ashley's head. "We'll have fun with this next time too." He said, holding up the silk tie before letting it fall to the ground. Ashley had already dropped his panties and was scooting back on the bed towards his wood-slatted headboard. When he was close enough, he reached over to his nightstand and pulling out lube and a box of condoms from the drawer. He felt the bed shift when Rick joined him on it.

He offered Rick the lube while he worked on opening the condom box. It would have been easier if his hands weren't shaking so much with anticipation. It had only been two nights since he'd had Rick inside his body, but still he missed it. Now that he was so close to being filled by Rick again, the excitement was boiling over.

While he was fumbling with the box, Rick had moved between his spread legs. Ashley removed a condom and tossed the box towards his nightstand. Rick had his hands under Ashley's thighs. He lifted Ashley's legs, pushing his knees towards his chest. "Hold them there." Rick commanded. Ashley quickly wrapped his arms behind his knees as Rick instructed. Using one hand, Rick lifted Ashley's hips so he could slide a pillow under his lower back.

He grabbed the lube and applied it to his fingers. Ashley moaned when they lightly circled his hole. Slowly slicking the ring before two fingers slipped inside. Rick didn't go fast, but instead, kept up a steady pressure until his fingers were completely inside. He left them there giving Ashley a chance to adjust to the welcome invasion.

"You can move. I'm not really that delicate." He said, encouraging Rick to get on with it. He really didn't need pampering, or slow and gentle. He had already made sure he was ready before heading to the Dairy Queen.

"Some things shouldn't be rushed." Rick responded, but started working his fingers back and forth inside Ashley.

Sighing, Ashley closed his eyes, simply enjoying the way Rick's fingers felt. However, he really wanted more. "There's a condom in my right hand when you're ready." He said, letting Rick know he was all set for taking this to the next level.

Rick took the condom from between Ashley's fingers as he removed his own fingers from Ashley's ass. Ashley heard the tearing of the packet and opened his eyes to watch Rick unroll the latex smoothly down his erection. He coated the condom in lube, and with one hand wrapped around the base of his shaft and the other on Ashley's thigh, he leaned forward aiming his cock at Ashley's prepared opening. Ashley sighed, as the pressure of Rick's hard dick forced his hole to stretch wider. He relaxed and let Rick slide in, enjoying the sensation of Rick filling him completely. With Rick fully inside, he let go of his legs and wrapped them around Rick's lower back, squeezing his legs together against Rick's back to make sure he was in as deep as possible. Rick fell forward, catching his weight on his arms, bringing them face to face before he slowly pulled his hips back and then thrust forward again.

He kept using shallow, slow strokes while he leaned down and planted another wet kiss on Ashley's lips. It was rough and grew messier as Rick started jerking his hips faster. Making longer, quicker strokes in and out of Ashley's body. The friction of Rick's stomach caressing his own erection was quickly bringing Ashley back to the edge. He was thankful he had already come or this would have been over much sooner. As it was, he was determined to hold off coming again until after Rick did.

Rick moved his head so that it rested on Ashley's shoulders as his pace grew more erratic. The grunts he was making let Ashley know he was getting close. A few thrusts later, Rick pushed all the way in and stayed there. Ashley knew by the way his body jerked a few times that he was coming. Reaching between their bodies, Ashley fisted his own cock, and with only a couple of strokes, he was joining Rick in sweet orgasmic ecstasy.

After catching their breath, they moved to the shower to get clean, which was actually more playful caressing touches than washing. They returned to Ashley's bed where they just cuddled together enjoying the post-coital euphoria. Ashley was unaware of how much time passed before Rick ruined the moment. "I should probably get going. I have to be at work in the morning, and I didn't bring clothes or anything with me."

"You should stay." Ashley was on his side, pressed up against Rick. He snuggled tighter into Rick's warm embrace. "We can call in sick and then you won't need any clothes."

"Mm, that is tempting." Rick sighed. Ashley had his one leg thrown over Rick's and he started rubbing his foot up and down Rick's calf. "I guess calling in for one day wouldn't hurt anything." Rick consented. Ashley smiled against his chest, pleased he wouldn't have to move and looking forward to spending tomorrow with Rick.

"I'll give you a blow job if you make me breakfast in bed." Ashley said cheekily.

"You would do that anyway."

"Right, but I'd do a better job on a fully nutritioned stomach."

"Do you even have food here to cook with?"

"I have milk and cereal." Ashley said yawning.

"You want me to pour you cereal and bring it to you in bed?" Rick asked unbelievingly.

"That'd be great, but not too early. I want to sleep in." Ashley closed his eyes and felt himself drifting off.

"Okay, Princess." Rick whispered quietly.

"Heard that." Ashley fell asleep with a smile on his lips.

Fluffy Stuff

A lot had changed since he started dating Rick. Even though they never officially said they were dating, they both agreed that they were ever since that first dinner at the Dairy Queen. They'd been back a few times since then. Ashley quickly learned about Rick's addiction to Oreo Blizzards. Though it had only been a few weeks, they'd spent most all of their free time together and quickly developed a comfortable companionship. It was more than just sexual, though the regular sex was a great benefit.

Not that it was *just* sex. It was more like amazing-everything-he'd-ever–wanted-in-a-partner sex. Toe curling, heart pounding, sweaty animal sex. The sex was truly great, but so were the moments just sitting on the couch watching television together. Usually with Ashley's feet in Rick's lap getting a deluxe foot massage. Dating a hottie with a foot fetish was awesome. Ashley's feet had never felt better, with Rick rubbing them nightly and regular moisturizer applications, they were soft and smooth. And with the better foot care, Ashley could wear his heels a lot longer with minimum discomfort. His feet had grown used to the pampering, so he really hoped Rick never got over his love of feet.

"You know, I've seen this episode before, and you're not really paying attention." Rick said, as he massaged Ashley's feet, which were nestled into his lap.

"Sorry, kind of got lost in my own thoughts." Ashley smiled at Rick. "What did I miss?"

"Nothing. And I was going to suggest we just turn it off and make our own entertainment for the rest of the night." He hesitated looking at Ashley worriedly, "Your smile is scaring me a little though, it looks too cheerful. What are you up to?"

"I was just thinking about how happy I've been lately. So if I look deliriously happy, well it's your fault." Ashley teased and stuck his tongue out, letting Rick see he was wearing the new stud Rick had gotten for him.

"In that case, I know a few ways to make tonight another memory for you to smile about." His tone was low and husky, the way it always got when Rick was excited. He moved Ashley's feet to rest on the couch cushion as he rose onto his knees. He leaned forward and slowly crawled over Ashley, his knees on the outside of Ashley's thighs, arms braced on either side of Ashley's head.

"I like this memory already." Ashley purred, looking into Rick's eyes and threading his fingers through Rick's soft hair. Rick leaned down and started kissing his way across Ashley's cheek, then brushing light, teasing kisses down his neck.

Before he got too deeply into it, he pulled back and looked down at Ashley, smiling. "We're just getting started. It will be a night to remember. Get up. It's time we started your cooking lessons." Rick pushed himself off the couch.

Ashley just stared at him for a second to see if he was serious. "You're a dirty tease. On second thought, I'd rather watch TV." He stretched his arm towards the coffee table reaching for the remote. Rick moved to block his attempt, so he tried shooing him away. "Seriously, I love that show."

"You don't even know what we were watching. The quicker we get through the lesson, the quicker we get to dessert. And trust me, you'll want dessert."

Ashley sighed and added extra effort into sitting up. "I can't believe I agreed to this. Better be one hell of an amazing dessert."

"You'll love every mouthwatering minute of it, I promise." Rick said, grinning. Ashley smiled back, knowing Rick always kept his word. *At the very least, this should make for one interesting night* Ashley thought to himself as he followed Rick into the kitchen. Ashley realized he was finally happy not having to have the last word. Even as much as he hated cooking, he couldn't muster any feelings of dread because he knew Rick would make the whole experience – amazing.

THE END

Author Bio

Kyle Adams started out dabbling with writing gay romance stories for fun. He writes what makes him laugh and hopes anyone who reads his work laughs with him. Kyle had two books nominated in the Goodreads M/M Romance Group 2012 reader's choice awards. He was nominated in the categories for Best Free Story and Best Humorous Story.

Kyle has a hard time picking a favorite anything (color, book, music, quote, et cetera), so trying to write a decent bio was quite the challenge. He is a very quiet person and is used to keeping things to himself. If there is anything you want to know, just ask.

Contact & Media Info

Kyle loves hearing from readers. Always feel free to contact him or add on any of the following:

Email | 2kyleadams@gmail.com

Blog | kyleadams2.com

www.ingramcontent.com/pod-product-compliance
Lightning Source LLC
Chambersburg PA
CBHW020423290526
45785CB00002B/692